Walking Alongside

Walking Alongside

A Theology for People-Helpers

BILL ANDERSEN

WIPF & STOCK · Eugene, Oregon

WALKING ALONGSIDE
A Theology for People-Helpers

Copyright © 2013 Bill Andersen. All rights reserved. Except for brief quotations in critical publications or reviews, no part of this book may be reproduced in any manner without prior written permission from the publisher. Write: Permissions. Wipf and Stock Publishers, 199 W. 8th Ave., Suite 3, Eugene, OR 97401.

Scripture taken from the Holy Bible, Today's New International Version™ TNIV® Copyright © 2001, 2005 by International Bible Society®. All rights reserved worldwide.

Wipf & Stock
An Imprint of Wipf and Stock Publishers
199 W. 8th Ave., Suite 3
Eugene, OR 97401

www.wipfandstock.com

ISBN 13: 978-1-62032-704-3

Manufactured in the U.S.A.

To Ruth
Before computers came, you typed and retyped my scripts: sometimes in clammy Sydney heat, sometimes in thawing London snows, sometimes near the soy-fields in Illinois. Your labor in the Lord was never lavished in vain. In memory of you, my dear joint-adventurer, this book is lovingly dedicated.

Contents

Foreword | ix
Acknowledgments | xi
Alongside: An Introduction | xiii

1 Counsel | 1
2 People | 18
3 Sin | 43
4 Self-Esteem | 61
5 Providence: Engagement by God | 75
6 Relationships | 91
7 Love | 113
8 Happiness | 123
9 Inwardness | 147
10 Profession | 172

Walking: An Epilogue | 191
Bibliography | 194

Foreword

Some books are the work of a moment. They sprout and flourish like weeds in a field but, being the product of little thought and less wisdom, they soon wither and die. They're fit to while away an idle moment in an airport or a waiting room somewhere, but bear little real fruit in thought or deed. And some authors seem to seed such books like dandelions seed weeds. Theirs is a world in which no thought goes unpublished, no matter how trivial.

Other books are the work of a lifetime, nourished by careful thought and deep wisdom. They may be a long time coming, but being the product of long reflection and rich experience, they repay the wait with fruit worth savoring. This is one such book.

Bill Andersen has long served the academy and the church as educator and philosopher and counselor. Having been claimed by the God of grace as a young man, he has lived out his love for God, and his commitment to the gospel of Christ by which God claimed him, in all that his hand has found to do. His life and thought have enriched the lives of countless women and men. I am one of many deeply indebted to his loving wisdom and clear-eyed faith. My wife and I remember him sitting with us over lunch while I was a brash young student (and he a key leader with many calls on his time), talking with us about our plans, encouraging me to see the life of the mind as a truly Christian calling. He gave us of his time and his wisdom—even though it meant being late for an important meeting. His is a commitment to people and their flourishing that wells up within him and cannot but flow in life-giving ways into their lives. This book is truly the work of a lifetime. I pray that it has the same kind of life-giving impact that Bill has had on me and many others.

This is also a book that reflects both thoughtful practice and theory brought to life. Now well into his eighties (and long "retired"—at least officially), Bill continues to serve as a counselor, bringing the light and

Foreword

wisdom of God to people struggling with brokenness, confusion, grief, and sin. His practice of counseling is informed by deep—and ongoing—reflection on Christian faith and good counseling theory and practice. And this is no accident.

For Bill, the gospel transforms everything: from minds and hearts to life and culture, and the theories that inform them. His view of the world and his engagement in it—from the counseling room to the work of Scripture Union (a movement he has contributed to for longer than I've been alive)—emerge from and seek to express the Father's embrace of us in the person of his Son and the transforming work of the Spirit who brings all things to fruition. But they do so, not in glorious isolation, quarantined from the "secular" academy and its challenges and insights, but in faithful and thoughtful conversation with them, seeking to bring all things—including the theory and practice of counseling—under the lordship of Jesus Christ. That's what this book demonstrates.

So, if you're looking for another evanescent product of Christian consumerism, a weedy little book that you can skim quickly in a waiting room and dispose of as quickly, then look elsewhere. This is not the book for you. But if you're after a product of long thought and deep wisdom, a book that engages the world of biblical thought and psychological theory, and wrestles hard to bring them together, then this is the book for you. But know this: it will require of you long thought; it will demand that you engage with the world of biblical thought and psychological theory; it will force you to wrestle hard to bring them together. If you do that, if you accept the invitation, then you stand to learn from Bill's great wisdom and, please God, acquire some for yourself.

Andrew Sloane,
October 2012

Acknowledgments

In the summer of 1967, I was captivated by the presentations, at a conference north of London, given by H.L. Ellison. His papers were: "Man [sic] in the Old Testament" and "Man in the New Testament." I thank Mr Ellison for seeding my interest in Biblical Anthropology. On return to Sydney University, Australia, that interest grew through part-time lecturing both at Morling (Baptist) College, and at Moore (Episcopalian) College, and was much enriched by their faculty members and libraries.

More contemporaneously, I acknowledge the debt to the editorial team at Wipf and Stock, and in particular, Rodney Clapp, Christian Amondson, and Diane Farley. You have been both kind and practically helpful to this stranger from "down under."

John Merchant, my pastor and friend, made available the contents of his expansive personal library, and also gave acute suggestions for relevant reading. These services he called his "investment."

Mark Street has been my mentor in the mysterious arts of word-processing, e-mailing, and printing. My moments of panic have been matched by his patient guidance and much-needed rescues.

When, after many interruptions, the text was complete, I sent it to four readers: Robert Banks, Terry Kohler, Andrew Sloane, and David Stewart. Most of their suggestions were followed. Their generosity in giving time to this task is deeply appreciated.

Neil Yorkston, on a brief trip from Canada, rubbished the original title I had devised for the book—in the friendliest possible way!—and caused the internal rumblings which led me to the present title.

To the Journal of Christian Education, represented by its current editor, Grant Maple, and its business manager, Austin Hukins, my thanks for authorising the modified use of several of my articles previously appearing in the Journal.

Acknowledgments

By no means the last in importance, my acknowledgements are gladly given to my copyeditor, Margaret Wilkins. Her immensely skilful work and helpful conversations have been such an encouragement.

Finally, while not wishing to be spiritually unctuous, I am compelled to record the "micro-providence" that has been clear and startling in so many stages of writing. This has been God's engagement with me. So the final word is "Praise!"

Alongside: An Introduction

It was arguably the most important Sunday afternoon walk that would ever occur. The two friends were disconsolate and confused, but they walked and talked seriously, with the events of recent days behind them and a retreat to their homes ahead. They had a fair knowledge of the Hebrew Scriptures and were clinging to a view of them which included the hope of a conquering political messiah.

A new hiker joined them, friendly but inquisitive. He asked them what they were discussing so seriously. The question itself brought them to a standstill and grief took them over momentarily.

The one called Cleopas started talking about Jesus, a prophet who was powerful both verbally and in action, but who had been handed over by the Jewish leaders to the Romans in power, sentenced, and then crucified. At least some of his followers thought he would release their people in some dramatic way from the yoke of the Romans. The outcome, however, was the other way around.

But this was only half the story. Some of Jesus' women followers had gone to the tomb that very morning, and returned saying that they had seen some angels but no body! The angels, however, had said that he was alive. And all of this was confirmed later by some of the men. It was amazing, confusing, but somehow not encouraging.

The new companion was, in fact, Jesus himself; incognito, resurrected that morning, and now seeking out two of his followers who were not part of the inner circle—the Eleven—but with whom he wanted to share things of great value. And this he did. Ranging right through the Old Testament, he interpreted for them what was said about himself throughout the Scriptures. Cleopas and friend were, at the same time, rebuked because they had not perceived from the Old Testament that the Messiah had to suffer before entering his glory.

Alongside: An Introduction

There is more of the story to come, but at this point an observation can be made.

The two were Jews with a tolerable knowledge of their Scriptures and a reasonable grasp of the socio-political situation of their day. Furthermore they had been living fairly close to Jesus and had had contact with others in the disciple-band. Still there were things that they had missed which were vital to their understanding of the whole picture. No doubt what Jesus told them was overwhelming, both in detail and in total impact, but it provided a new lens—a transformed view—both of King and of kingdom. And this they would now take into their future work of whatever kind, not solely as information, but as an enhanced part of themselves and their attitudes.

A clear scriptural and theological perspective can, even in our day and circumstances, act as *a presupposition* lying behind or beneath whatever thought and activity recruit our hands and our hearts. It can provide an "infrastructure" to sustain a viable system or manner of approach. None of this is intended to imply that any present-day scholarly or devotional survey would approach the wonder, penetration, or completeness of Jesus' exposition, but it is appropriate, just the same, to attempt a biblical undergirding for our normal jobs, worked out to the best of our ability, in reliance upon the Spirit of Jesus.

Our story continues. When the three were getting close to Emmaus, the two friends—possibly husband and wife—gave a strong invitation to their fellow-traveler to come in with them for supper. He agreed, but at the table acted rather more like a host than a guest: the hint of a gracious authority. Then, whatever the reason, they recognized him. It was Jesus! Suddenly, at that moment, he was gone.

Rather than indulging in disappointment, they now reflected jointly on their experience during the walk. No doubt in the hours that they had walked and talked, they had been becoming aware of something unusual happening to them. But now, on reflection, the intensity of what had happened came to them irresistibly. *Their hearts had been burning within them* while Jesus talked and opened the Scriptures. They had been deeply moved, in their totality, not only by the light shed on their Scriptures but also by the person who had chosen to walk alongside, to be with them. Fresh understanding had been riveting; but it had been clothed with Presence and accompanied with an inner fiery drive.

Those Christians who walk alongside others to help them will, then, take account of the two momentous discoveries in the Emmaus story. There

Alongside: An Introduction

are *biblical truths which are an indispensible lens through which to view afresh all of our helping processes;* and my purpose is to contribute a degree of relevant understanding to some of these. Also there is *Jesus, himself,* who yearns to come alongside the helper to guide, challenge, support, and convey a practical love towards those he called "the least of these brothers and sisters of mine": those with whom he identified.

It is this kind of vision which has structured the approach of this book. It does not attempt to provide a new theory of counseling into which biblical insights have been integrated, or of the other helping disciplines. Such a task is inviting and would be exciting but that is not what has been attempted here. Also, no claim is made that these insights cover the full range of any discipline. Those discussed seem to me to be important but others, perhaps equally important, might well be added. This can be seen, then, as "a work in progress."

Chapter 1, while necessarily setting the scene, spells out some indicators of the Bible's approach to the notion of *"counsel"* and also what current readers would recognize as *"counseling."*

Chapter 2 is written recognizing that *the understanding of people, or of one person*, is absolutely basic for any approach to *helping* people. Hence the chapter looks through the lens provided by Christian Scripture in its use of *person-words*, even though these are not pursued systematically within the Bible. Here are insights not to be missed, which may also serve as a corrective for some contemporary assumptions.

Chapter 3 confronts us with the topic that periodically becomes lost to sight in our academic discussions about human beings: *the nature of sin.* Sin is to be distinguished from antisocial behavior and unfortunate conditioning. It intrudes into counseling and other processes more often than many of us would be prepared to admit; but since it is there, it is important to deal with it, in the whole economy of the personality involved.

Chapter 4 completes our treatment of persons by selecting out *the question of self-esteem*, which has been pushed to the forefront of discussion in recent decades. It looks, first, at New Testament data in some detail and then at a Puritan view of self, exposing both the strengths and weaknesses of the latter approach. Finally it brings to bear insights from these sources upon the current scene.

Chapter 5 switches attention from human beings to God. It looks at *the ways in which God is actively dealing with his creatures and working in their lives*, whether or not they recognize this. Its interest is chiefly in those

Alongside: An Introduction

who are not as yet committed to following God or his anointed one. To be *expecting* this activity of God is bound to make a difference from the way we discern things and are motivated in approach as helpers.

Chapter 6 concerns itself with *the nature of relationships*: a major revelation made clear through the new lens. Here relationships, which are basic for the understanding of Scripture as a whole, are also basic for the understanding of human beings; the overlap is considerable. The Trinity is involved, as are the links of a personal kind among individuals. Attention is given to some theoretical issues and particularly to empirical studies of relationships between counselors and clients.

Chapter 7 is a logical extension of the previous chapter in that, while the treatment is still connected with relationships, here the focus is on *the ideal quality of relationships: "love,"* for which the Greek term in the New Testament is *agape*. The inference that the helper should love the client requires an unpacking of the meaning of love which reveals it to be considerably more than a romantic or insipid attachment.

Chapter 8 deals critically with the assertion that the primary purpose of life is the pursuit of happiness. It explores the biblical nuances of terms such as "happiness," "blessedness," and "joy," and then extends its treatment to several major philosophical approaches, as well as to the recent emphasis on Positive Psychology. It is a central issue *whether counseling and other helping processes do or should take aim at the pursuit of happiness*, in whatever guise that may appear.

Chapter 9 is concerned with *the inner personal experiences of the client and whether these can be employed to bring about a fruitful outcome*. Though Christian faith is by no means confined to inner experience, the Bible does document such lavishly. The current emphasis on "mindfulness" in counseling is also explored, particularly in view of its recent association both with Buddhist practices and also with neuroscience.

Chapter 10, entitled "Profession," treats *the ways in which a person professing Christian faith may express that faith within counseling in particular, while at the same time taking account of the codes of ethics* produced by those bodies which supervise the counseling profession. (The two senses of "profession" are deliberately juxtaposed!) There exists a twofold responsibility then: first to Christ's command and also to the governance of one's society, as was also the case in the days of Jesus and Paul.

It remains to say that these presuppositions underlying the practice of counseling by a Christian are both very broad and very selective. Hopefully

Alongside: An Introduction

their very breadth will prevent them from turning into a set of blinkered rules. It is hoped, as they become basic and even burning attitudes, that their contribution will be recognized. They have been selected for a variety of reasons: partly because some have *not* been widely recognized to this point; partly because some *do* relate to issues that are currently receiving much attention within counseling and other circles; but largely because of *the close connections,* identified throughout the book, between the concerns of God-sight and human-aid.

1

Counsel

The "helping professions" include doctors, social workers, occupational therapists, counselors, and many more. What is in common is, by and large, the idea of *restoring* clients or patients to a "normal" or acceptable state of wellbeing. Closely allied are the endeavors of educationists, except that these are concerned mainly with *building* the resources of people through learning and experience. Nor are these two groups mutually exclusive, for there will often be elements of teaching included in counseling and medicine; and these, in turn, will be called upon to deal with certain personal problems that are preventing the person from learning in the usual way. Biblically, both the restorers and the equippers join in the task of "doing good" to the people they serve.

In the light of this, the question could be posed: what does the Bible have to say about the spirit and the conduct of medicine, social work, dietetics and, especially, counseling—along with psychology, which is thought to act as its major scientific base? And, furthermore, if counseling and social work can be seen as forms of "doing good," would we expect them to differ, when applied to believers, from the way they would operate when applied to unbelievers?

Within situations such as medicine, social work, and counseling where many profess an interest in the person-as-a-whole, the area of overlap or common interest with the Bible is considerable; for what can be discerned from biblical sources is that persons are seen as many-faceted beings in view of the many kinds of relationships they enter upon. And while, at this point, the aim is not to list the central areas of biblical contribution, it can be acknowledged in reference to both Testaments that the personal ideology or world view of the individual is all-of-a-piece with his or her orientation in life: *where* he or she "looks," and *to what* he or she is committed; and this is of common concern both to the helper and to the biblical student.

A. AN APPROPRIATE RESPONSE BY CHRISTIANS TO THE QUESTION OF OVERLAP?

One reaction, formulated several decades ago by Jay Adams, was that there is no such category as *psychological* problems; there are only *physical* problems and *spiritual* problems. Asked by one of the authors of a carefully researched book on Christianity and psychology if he had any words of guidance for Christians studying psychology, Adams responded thus:

> Drop out of graduate school. If you want to serve God as a counselor, you can only do so by going to seminary, studying the Word of God rather than the words of men, and becoming a pastor.[1]

But if there are no psychological problems, then what is one to say about the person whose leg is paralyzed, but for whose condition the most searching medical tests can establish no physical basis? Or for the infant who, though given appropriate exercise and nourishment, nevertheless languishes and dies for lack of relational warmth? Or for the teenager who breaks out aggressively against peers and teachers at school, because he observes his parents fighting each night at home? In the latter case we could draw attention to the youngster's sin of angry aggression, and this might need to be cautiously admitted. But if we neglected the psychological effects of his parents' aggression upon his developing personality, observed systematically and scientifically by groups of psychologists, we would be ignoring a human reality, and thus neglecting our duty of care.

The opposite reaction would be for the "scientific Christian" to claim that the whole sphere of human reactions will be clarified only by careful research, and that it is best to leave biblical import to "spiritual concerns" such as public and private worship. Psychological cure could be achieved only as the ways of our organism, seen through the connections between stimuli and responses, are progressively unraveled. Christian "do-gooders" are likely to muddy the waters.

---

1. Jones and Butman, *Modern Psychotherapies*, 18.

But this view also is clearly unacceptable, for the Bible says so much on persons-in-community, on communication, on sin, and on orientation, that to ignore all this in therapy would be close to admitting that the gospel is a purely theoretical construct and has no practical impact on the real world of people, society, and culture.

Another possible reaction is the one outlined by Lawrence Crabb in *Effective Biblical Counseling*, where he recognizes "we can profit from secular psychology if we carefully screen our own concepts to determine their compatibility with Christian presuppositions."[2]

Such screening is likely, given not only theological *concepts* but also a theological *cast of mind*. Granted this screening, we can allow our helping approach to be structured by all that we glean from biblical sources and, indeed, from theology more inclusively; but equally we need not baulk at including all evidence-based knowledge from medical, psychological, and sociological sources. It is true that, in detail, the latter will not supply final answers, because any empirical study may be modified or changed over time. We can only be required to act in the light of the information available to us at any one time, and we shall make mistakes; but we will at least be strengthened by an understanding of revealed truth at the core of our approach.

At this point, we refer to the biblical text:

> Therefore, as we have opportunity, let us do good to all people, especially to those who belong to the family of believers. (Gal 6:10 TNIV)[3]

Two practical issues arise. First, if believers need help through counseling, and manifestly many of them do—they are by no means exempt—how important is it that they be counseled by another believer? A little earlier we claimed, "it has to be acknowledged that the personal ideology or world view of the individual is all-of-a-piece with his or her orientation in life." And this is as true, of course, for the counselor as for the counselee. Hence it is all too possible that the counselor who is not a believer will get a quite different slant on a problem from a counselee who is. The counselor may admit or deny factors differently but, of more importance, will make significant judgments on a different basis.

---

2. Crabb, *Effective Biblical Counseling*, 48.

3. Scripture quotations are taken from the TNIV unless otherwise noted, with italics added for emphasis where pertinent.

Walking Alongside

The prime example, of course, is the consistent Freudian who may well encourage the release of sexual "inhibitions" from the overriding taboos of society and will be prepared, if necessary, to ride roughshod over Christian sexual and marital ethics. On the other side, to be fair, is what I shall call the "faith-only Christian" who advises fellow believers to banish physical or mental illness solely through faithful prayer. Wherever possible, then, it seems advisable for the believer to be counseled by another believer; assuming, of course, that the latter is well-trained and competent in the practice of counseling, as well as being grounded in an ample knowledge of the Scriptures, along with those principles of interpretation which help to establish their meaning.

However, as intimated already, there needs to be balance in implementing the preference expressed above. Consider the case of being operated upon for a serious heart complaint by a dedicated fellow believer who is as yet inexperienced in this aspect of surgery! One must acknowledge that some counselors who are not believers do seem able to respect the orientation of their client and leave it intact, as it were. And cases are evident in which measures have been taken which were decidedly helpful, having been drawn, as through "common grace," from what is helpful to any human being in the circumstances.

Second, is it possible for a Christian counselor to give genuine help to an unbeliever? Jay Adams says "No!"; the very first step is to evangelize him or her. Once again we have to disagree with Adams. For reasons sketched in the paragraph above, there are therapeutic procedures at hand which can yield genuine outcomes to the non-Christian client, even in the absence of faith. Facing up to reality, rather than running away from it, is one. Learning to listen to one's spouse, rather than merely blaming them, is another! At least an *improvement* in these skills may be brought about; and if this is so, not only has the Christian counselor "done good" for the client, but by showing concern and perhaps making some modest reference, if in context, to their Christian faith, a witness may have been given. But this is a far cry from the "evangelism" that Adams had in mind and also is a factor *within* the process of counseling, rather than *preceding* it. (For a further elaboration of this point, see chapter 10.) And, in addition, Christian counselors must be able to respect the current orientation of their non-Christian clients.

For Adams there is a logical difficulty in counseling the non-Christian. In contrast, however, we discern a challenge to service, even if this amounts only to applying a "band-aid" or a "tourniquet"; though also, in this relational context, there is the likelihood of showing Christ's love. Here is one disquieting fact. Sometimes a Christian client has been less willing to face reality, or to listen to his or her spouse, than a non-Christian client! This is a warning not to be over-strident, within counseling, about expected differences between the responses of Christians and those of non-believers.

B. A BIBLICAL MEANING FOR "COUNSEL"?

We referred earlier to the connection between "education" on the one hand and "helping professions" on the other. Counseling, as an example, would be seen generally as *restoring* clients to a normal state of wellbeing, whereas education would be seen generally as *building* the resources of people. It is now possible to ask whether there are biblical concepts which correspond with the English terms "to educate" or "to counsel."

In reply, it seems that there is no biblical term which covers exactly what we mean by the English verb "to educate." The Greek word *paideuo* comes somewhat near it, but is geared rather too much towards "discipline." *Oikodomeo* also comes close, when rendered "upbuild," but is scarcely specific enough or sufficiently developmental. However, the way in which we spell out education will, for the Christian, be permeated by the spirit of upbuilding and modified, perhaps, by the need to incorporate discipline. Thus while it is not possible to identify "education" strictly as a biblical concept, it is certainly possible to give it a direction and a flavor that is distinctively Christian rather than neutral or humanistic.

And similarly with "counseling."

1. Old Testament

The basic Hebrew word is *yo'es*, which is translated "counselor," "adviser," or "encourager." Counsel may come from the Lord or a friend (Prov 27:9); or from someone like Ahithophel, who was anything but a friend to David (2 Sam 15: 31); or the wicked, or virtually anyone. "Counselor" in the "royal" passage referring to God (Isa 9:6) is also *yo'es* though, tantalizingly, the qualities of the counseling function are not spelled out.

In Isaiah 40:13, the word translated "counselor" is *esahl*. Once again the translations of *esahl* include "advice," as in *yo'es*, but then tend in the direction of "plans," "purposes," "schemes," "strategy," "decisions," and "consultations." Now Isaiah 40:13–14 reads as follows:

> Who can fathom the mind (or Spirit) of the LORD,
> or instruct the LORD as his counselor?
> Whom did the LORD consult to enlighten him,
> and who taught him the right way?

Ignoring the intended irony of the passage within its literary context, it is interesting that counseling is associated with fathoming, or directing, or enlightening someone with an ethical aim in view. Also of interest is that "Spirit" or "mind" (*ruach*), in the Hebrew idiom, indicates deep-seated identity. It is implied that to instruct or enlighten someone, we must fathom or understand who the particular person is. This reference, then, comes close to our current notion that a counselor is someone who gets to know the one being counseled at close quarters, and who then may speak in the light of that relationship. This is not to suggest that our current concept is *identical* to a biblical term, but merely that there is a notable degree of overlap.

2. New Testament

In the New Testament, "counselor" is one of the translations of *parakletos*, the other principal one being "someone called in defense," perhaps a lawyer or advocate. The literal meaning of the term is "one who is called alongside" presumably to help or support. The word occurs in 1 John 2:1, where it refers to Christ, the one who speaks in our defense, in a quasi-legal sense. It also occurs in John's Gospel 14:26; 15:26, and 16:7, where the references are to the Holy Spirit. In each case the Counselor is a permanent companion who, in two of the passages, brings truth, and in the third, proves the world to be in the wrong about sin, and righteousness, and judgment. Without straining translation or interpretation, the *parakletos* is one who is called alongside with the tasks of supporting, teaching, and "plumbing the depths" personally, especially in an ethical way.

Paraklesis, the noun, is translated "encouragement" and "comfort." Barnabas is the "son of *paraklesis*." And there is a general exhortation in Romans 12:8—If [your gift] is to encourage, then give encouragement. Thus *paraklesis* is described as a gift.

These uses of the verb and the noun stand within the general tradition of *yo'es* and *esahl* in the Old Testament and would be part of the role of most Christians who might well provide comfort and encouragement to their fellow-believers. The Johannine use of *parakletos*, while referring exclusively to Christ and the Holy Spirit, has features which are strongly reminiscent of the role of a human counselor as we conceive it today. An important link between divine and human counselors is implicit in what has already been noted above: that encouragement or comfort is a gift of the *Paraclete* who activates his concerns through the identity and actions of those whom he inhabits.

Just as in the case of "education" our limited Christian claim was that the process will be permeated by a spirit of upbuilding; so, in the case of counseling, our limited claim will be that the whole process will be permeated by a desire to come alongside the client with the aim of coming to know him or her at a personal level; and further, that presence, support, and challenge will be offered.

C. OUR CENTRAL QUEST

1. What is the point of counseling?

Our goal, at this point, is to work towards a usable form of belief for Christians engaged in counseling. This, however, is not merely a pleasant academic or theoretical pastime. Every practical pursuit and, in particular, every helping profession draw definition and quality of action from certain presuppositions. Often practitioners are not conscious of these and seldom are they clearly articulated. Our conviction is that underneath the believer's counseling actions and attitudes there lie presuppositions of a Christian kind that need to be spelled out, consciously recognized, and embraced, at least as a challenge, by those who find themselves both disciples and counselors.

This journey of discovery will take a number of twists and turns before the pattern will become clear. To start, however, we need to look in somewhat more detail at *what contemporary counseling is*. Many of us may feel that this is a simple thing to define or describe because we have undergone counseling ourselves, or because we know people close to us who have, and hence we may have an intuitive notion drawn from our own experience. And this is not to be altogether despised. However, in a search within the current climate for a more objective answer we find that counseling is often equated with either therapy or personal change. If therapy, i.e., healing, there will be the need to ask *what we or others are to be healed from*? If, instead, we follow the line of change in persons, then the question arises, *what kind of change* should we pursue? Shall we need to distinguish, for example, between change for the better and change for the worse? And if so, *what norms or criteria shall we use to decide*?

It is in fact very difficult to discover authors, writing about counseling, who are ready to be decisive or clear on these issues. Roger P. Greenberg makes this straightforward statement: "The objective in therapy is *to alleviate patient distress*" (my emphases).[4]

Greenberg's suggestion must be granted considerable respect, since it obviously carries intuitive weight, but at least two issues need to be considered. First, one could suggest that some people come for counseling when undecided or puzzled about some issue in life, but without any marked distress; and indeed this would fit in with older notions of counsel as the proffering of advice. A second and more important issue is whether distress should always be alleviated! This may seem to be a heartless thing to say and one lacking in compassion. But one must pause to ask whether distress or suffering is not at times a very good teacher; and this point will be taken up for discussion in chapter 2. Hence, even from the starting point of a supposedly simple and plausible statement, there can be important ramifications.

2. Diversity in counseling

It is common knowledge that there are literally hundreds of different approaches to counseling within the USA alone, to say nothing of those generated in other countries. And this is not the end of the matter. New forms of therapy or counseling appear almost daily on the American or the international scene. Furthermore they vary enormously both in terms of their basic rationale, and the therapeutic procedures which flow from it. There are still those, for example, who counsel on a Freudian basis, using much of the original rationale but with somewhat changed procedures. At the same time there are those—many indeed—who counsel from the viewpoint of Cognitive Behavioral Therapy, this having been for quite some time a strongly preferred approach. Many other examples are available, but these two have been chosen because they are in such stark contrast.

What, then, characterizes counseling at any one time? Are we forced into a position where all that we can do is to speak of particular counseling modes rather than counseling in general? But, in fact, we often do speak of

---

4. Greenberg, "Common Psychsocial Factors," 317.

counseling in general! Our newspapers and television reports frequently refer to people who have suffered awful shocks or experienced dreadful trauma and who are therefore "offered counseling." But what does this offer actually mean, when the whole area is characterized by multiple alternatives and considerable confusion? A way out is pursued in section D of this chapter.

3. "Christian counseling"

Sometimes it is assumed, or even advertised, that Christian counseling is one particular type of counseling, in much the same way as we discerned Freudian or Cognitive Behavioral Counseling to be. Thus, by implication, "Christian Counseling" is seen to be one competitor among a number of others, and one which Christians would be expected to seek as a priority. In this way "Christian Counseling" would take its place alongside "Christian Education" as a different and preferable kind of service offered. There may be some plausibility in claiming that the services, offered to people under Christian auspices, can be called "Christian" as distinct from others that are not so-called, but there are many minefields which lie in the path of this interpretation, if pressed indiscriminately.

For the moment, we shall be content to describe Christian counseling as the counseling carried out by knowledgeable and experienced Christians. Our assumption is that such people have taken the trouble to study the whole field, if possible along with one of its basic disciplines such as psychology or sociology, and also to have acquired appropriate skills. In brief, *Christian counseling is counseling carried out by appropriately trained Christians.* And this characterization is seen to be completely in accord with Crabb's statement quoted in section A of this chapter: "we can profit from secular psychology if we carefully screen our concepts to determine their compatibility with Christian presuppositions." Such counseling, then, can and should be *eclectic*, drawing from the whole range of appropriate knowledge, while maintaining a distinctive rationale, with biblical theology as its undergirding.

4. A theology of counseling

Why is it necessary for Christians to envisage a *theology* of counseling? Is it that theologians have a passion for theologizing everything? If there can be satisfactory services helping humankind in the form of medicine, surgery,

Walking Alongside

and dentistry, which appear to get along excellently in a purely secular context, then why not a thoroughly secular understanding of counseling? In attempting to answer this question, we must have a clear look at the task of theology. Though delineating this task is itself a controversial point, it is nevertheless pertinent to note the lucid statement of Stanley J. Grenz in his book, *The Social God and the Relational Self*:

> Theology's *critical* task entails examining beliefs and teachings about God and the world in the light of the sources of the Christian faith. Its *constructive* task, in turn, involves portraying Christian beliefs as a comprehensive, coherent whole, as well as relating the Christian belief mosaic faithfully and relevantly to contemporary culture.[5]

Though Grenz's goal is to display Christian beliefs as "a comprehensive, coherent whole," he cheerfully admits that it is not possible for the Christian faith to be formed into a tightly knit and completely logical system. Hence comprehensiveness and coherence would always be matters of degree. The exciting task of theologians, therefore, is to find multiple interconnections within the subject matter, drawing initially from Scripture, and then proceeding to extrapolate beyond through a variety of other insights congruent with it. The powerful and challenging thing, however, from our viewpoint is the second element in Grenz's statement, that of *relating the Christian belief mosaic faithfully and relevantly to contemporary culture*. What this amounts to is putting theology to work!

In his previous systematic work entitled, *Theology for the Community of God*, Grenz deals first with theology as the doctrine of God in which God himself is seen as a community of love. Next he deals with what theologians call "anthropology," the doctrine of humanity, which incorporates approximately what a secular university would include as psychology, sociology, anthropology, and ethics.

The two doctrines are clearly related because God in his creation was concerned to be connected personally to human beings as creatures capable of reciprocating his outgoing love. The Bible, in fact, and the theology flowing from it say a tremendous amount on the subject of humankind (see chapter 2). In the case of most biblical authors this is quite unsystematic, but nonetheless highly significant. It is, therefore, from biblical and theological anthropology that contributions may be anticipated to counseling and therapy. Interestingly also, these sources regularly emphasize issues of

---

5. Grenz, *The Social God*, ix. My emphases.

relationship and also, within this context, issues of *ethical connection*. The latter is in some contrast with most of the twentieth century's psychology, which tended to react to ethical questions as a contamination of any rigorous view of human beings and their personalities.

5. Counseling within contemporary Western culture

So far we have been etching a brief case for counseling as an aspect of what Grenz calls "constructive theology." Now, however, we look in another direction and ask: what role does counseling play in contemporary efforts to assist human beings cope with their circumstances? It is now well recognized in the Western world that, whereas mentoring and the giving of advice were once the tasks of priests and pastors, they have now effectively become the tasks of counselors. In fact, lines of demarcation have been formulated whereby pastors may deal with "religious" or moral matters, but when issues go more deeply in an intrapersonal or interpersonal direction, then they should hand the parishioner over to a professionally trained counselor after, perhaps, four or five "pastoral" sessions.

It is at this point that an ideological issue intrudes. If the counselor is a Christian, then they will deal with issues that, for the client, involve God, or the relationships between people, as seen in the light of God's self-revelation. Indeed the Christian counselor will, if consistent, bring a Christian interpretation of life to any of the dilemmas presented by clients. Of course this does not mean that every issue has a predetermined Christian solution. That would be facile, but also dangerous, because neither the Bible, nor the theology emerging alongside it, is meant to cover every human issue in detail.

The situation is, however, that counselors of non-Christian persuasion will similarly carry some ideology to *their* professional work which either influences or even permeates it, and which brings to bear *some* interpretation of life and the world upon the dilemmas of their clients. This is not to say that such a process is a bad thing! We have all profited from the wisdom of Christians and non-Christians alike in many personal and social matters and, as mentioned before, this is something that theologians might well include under "common grace." *Counseling, then, is theoretically or ideologically tinged*, and is as potentially influenced by world-view notions, formulated or intuitive, as is any other practice involving the welfare of human beings.

Walking Alongside

In the Western world, psychology has assumed the predominant place in the determination of counseling theory and practice. Somewhat grudgingly, sociology has been admitted and, along with it, social work. More recently, Buddhist teachings and practices have been included. We have been arguing here that Christian theology be recognized within the list of serious contributors. In this connection, we refer to a particular contribution from Stanley Grenz, whose chapter 2, in *The Social God and the Relational Self*, entitled "From Interiority to Psychotherapy: An Archaeology of the Self" is a brilliant survey of relevant thought commencing with the fourth century and extending to the present.

D. THE MANY THERAPIES

At the beginning of the twentieth century there is no doubt that Sigmund Freud held the stage, so far as psychotherapy was concerned. In spite of defections by his earlier colleagues, Carl Jung and Alfred Adler, the dominance of his thinking within the field was strong and long-lasting. Shortly after his death in 1939, however, his own daughter Anna Freud infused the social environment into her father's doctrines, and the Neo-Freudian movement had begun. This initiative, however, appeared to unleash a number of others which were to move further and further away from the old orthodoxy. And then commenced a flood of new therapies, whose emphases went in every direction imaginable. It is not part of our present purpose to identify these movements, but rather to point to their abundance, their sheer diversity, and in some cases, their cult-like nature. Some, particularly that produced by Carl Rogers, (for example, in his book *Client-Centered Therapy*) which at first he had called "non-directive," tended to hold the field for quite a number of years, in a way reminiscent of the Old Master. But once again the rebels in the therapeutic world got to work and many more therapies were defined, some being reactions from their notable predecessors.

1. Organizing the deluge

What was to be done about this vast proliferation of viewpoints?

Much time was spent in attack and defense, and great amounts of money in advertisement and self-promotion, particularly in institutions concerned with the teaching of counseling. In view of the large and ever-growing number of "denominations" was the stage being set for an

"Ecumenical Movement"? Perhaps something of that kind! In the late 1980s there assembled a large and prestigious gathering of therapy-originators at a historic conference sponsored by J.K. Zeig and others who had had a strong association with the talented and dedicated hypnotherapist, Milton Erickson. The conference had been convened in time for a number of the "ageing greats" to attend, and a book emerged with the polite title, *The Evolution of Psychotherapy*.[6] Since "evolution" indicates at least some form of continuous development, the title was a misnomer. The various songs were sung and the discords made apparent; but little harmony ensued.

A decade later, a serious and painstaking effort was made to evaluate the effectiveness of various therapeutic approaches to many of the major disturbances in human personality and behavior. P.E. Nathan and J.M. Gorman produced a substantial volume called *Treatments That Work*. This was certainly an approach to be respected and one of the first, on a large scale, to present a critical evaluation which was organized from the viewpoint of the sufferer, rather than that of the therapist. Its task was to sift out the valuable or the promising from the merely faddish.

2. A Christian contribution

In the meantime, there appeared a most interesting work in the form of a book titled *Modern Psychotherapies* by S.L. Jones and R.E. Butman. The authors had, first of all, selected a number of highly influential models of therapy—a demanding task in itself—and then had critiqued each of these, first in the light of the psychological evidence available at the time; and then by giving a Christian evaluation both of the underlying rationale involved and also the emergent treatments. Their approach was well-balanced, in the sense that they would stretch themselves to find ways of commending aspects in each of the psychotherapies first, before expressing negative criticisms. What this involved, among other things, was a recognition of insights reflecting some aspects of the biblical approach to human beings, even when in "secular dress"; or at least aspects which, while not directly biblical, were certainly *not foreign* to a biblical approach. The book was not only impeccable, from the viewpoint of psychological study and understanding, but was also philosophically and theologically sophisticated. It remains, along with its successor, *Modern Psychopathologies* by M.A. Yarhouse, R.E.

---

6. Zeig, ed., *The Evolution of Psychotherapy*.

Butman, and B.W. McRay, a remarkable example of thorough and practical Christian scholarship.

3. A radically new perspective

In 1999 there appeared upon the scene an explosive new "secular" approach—from the extreme "left field"—to the issue of therapeutic denominationalism, in a volume entitled, *The Heart and Soul of Change* by M.A. Hubble, B.L. Duncan, and S.D. Miller. The approach of the authors was to seek out, by very careful survey and research, the factors that were *common* to the vast array of therapies and to differentiate them from the factors that were *specific* to particular approaches. The process had involved the coming together of interested people including, of course, the three authors, but others in addition. In due course there appeared a number of journal articles, based on careful and rigorous research and analysis, and finally the book itself.

The authors recall an amazing challenge brought to the whole therapeutic community by the rather quirky British psychologist, Hans Eysenk.

> Eysenk, the great gadfly to the advocates of therapy, slammed the mental health professions for their ineffectiveness during the 1950s and 1960s. Through his analyses of outcome research, he claimed that approximately two thirds of all clients, bearing a diagnosis of neurosis, substantially improved within two years of entering therapy. He also claimed that an equal number or proportion of clients, also labeled neurotic, improved within a comparable period without therapy . . . This inauspicious, unfavorable assessment ignited a firestorm of debate and long put the medical health professions on the defensive.[7]

The first response to this challenge was to carry out extensive surveys to check on Eysenk's conclusion. To cut a long story short, these surveys indicated that Eysenk was basically wrong and that, in fact, *therapy works!* And this, of course, is a highly significant finding, whatever the theoretical context. The second response, however, involved a question: how was it that approaches of such wide diversity would all result in some beneficial effects, when there were so many mutually contradictory trends among them, both in rationale and treatment? It is to this question that Hubble

---

7. Hubble et al., *The Heart and Soul of Change*, 1.

and his associates directed their investigation, and to which we now turn our detailed attention.

4. Results

The research established that there are four factors involved in successful therapy, the first three of which are *common*, though varying in significance, and the last of which is *specific* to particular therapeutic approaches.

First are "Client/Extratherapeutic Factors" which account for 40 percent of total outcome variance! The authors describe this as follows:

> These factors, unquestionably the most common and powerful of the common factors in therapy, are part of the client or the client's life circumstances that aid in recovery despite the client's formal participation in therapy.[8] They consist of the client's strengths, supportive elements in the environment, and even chance events. In short, they are what clients bring to the therapy room and what influences their lives outside. As examples of these factors, persistence, faith, a supportive grandmother, membership in a religious community, sense of personal responsibility, a new job, a good day at the tracks, a crisis successfully managed; all may be included.[9]

(Note that what influences the lives of clients in ordinary experience will be discussed in chapter 5, which deals with Providence.)

The second of the three common factors is described as "Relationship Factors." The importance of such factors has long been noted, in a purely anecdotal way, by many therapists. The authors claim, however, that this class of factors accounts for 30 percent of the successful outcome variance. Once again, a highly significant finding! Their comments on this factor follow:

> These represent a wide range of relationship-mediated variables found among therapies no matter the therapist's theoretical persuasion. Caring, empathy, warmth, acceptance, mutual affirmation, and encouragement of risk taking and mastery are but a few. Except what the client brings to therapy, these variables are

---

8. It seems likely that these are the factors Eysenk had stumbled upon—my interpretation, not that of the authors.
9. Ibid., 9.

probably responsible for most of the gains resulting from psychotherapy interventions.[10]

(These factors will be discussed in chapters 6 and 7, dealing respectively with Relationships and Love.)

The third of the three common factors is described as "Placebo, Hope, and Expectancy," accounting for 15 percent of total therapeutic outcome. The authors' comment follows:

> In successful therapies both client and therapist believe in the restorative power of the treatment's procedures or rituals. These curative effects therefore are not thought to derive specifically from a given treatment procedure; they come from the positive and hopeful expectations that accompany the use and implementation of the method.[11]

The main factor being described here is *hope*! Yes, it does involve what the authors indicate as mutual affirmation, by client and therapist, in whatever treatment is being undertaken; but it also embraces the reality, known alike to the psychological and the medical professions, of the placebo factor. This factor is not to be despised or discounted, but to be seen in the context of the part played by hope in the life of any person. In its turn, hope or expectancy implies active looking forward rather than immersion in the past. Needless to say, this factor, as with previous common factors, is full of theological connotations!

The fourth element contributing to the therapeutic variance is called "Model/Technique Factors." These are seen also to contribute 15 percent of the final outcome.

Research continues to be done within particular therapeutic approaches and some individual techniques are emerging as helpful in particular circumstances. According to the authors these include:

> ... the miracle question in solution-focused brief therapy, the use of the genogram in Bowen-oriented family therapy, hypnosis, systematic desensitisation, biofeedback, transference interpretations, and the respective theoretical premises attending these practices.[12]

In addition, later in their book, the authors acknowledge the rather widely accepted finding that cognitive behavioral therapy has particular

---

10. Hubble et al., *The Heart and Soul of Change*, 9.
11. Ibid., 10.
12. Ibid., 10.

efficacy with respect to a number of conditions, including depression. It is interesting, however, that this fashionable therapy does not take first place among the specific variables mentioned.

These are certainly revolutionary findings! In particular, what they do is to encourage efforts to meet the requirements of the common factors in counseling, without neglecting specific variables in the process. *The Heart and Soul of Change* has provided an open door to all therapists who seek significance rather than notoriety in their concern for their clients, and this certainly should include those with a theological orientation.

5. Conclusion and transition

Much terrain has been traversed in this chapter. First, we have presented a view that the Christian presupposition within counseling is a call to come alongside the client to know him or her at a personal level, and then to offer presence, support, and challenge. Second, we have displayed a brief—and, no doubt, selective—history of counseling in the twentieth century, highlighting the divergence among "schools" which have developed. Finally, we have expounded the work of Hubble and his colleagues which yields an analysis of *common* factors in counseling as distinct from factors *specific* to a particular approach.

We have now discerned connections (a) between Hubble's "Client/Extratherapeutic Factors" and the biblical notion of "Providence" (see chapter 5); and (b) between Hubble's "Relationship Factors" and biblical teachings on Relationships and Love (see chapters 6 and 7).

However, before pursuing these issues, it is necessary to spell out what the Bible says about *people*: their structure, characteristics, and incorporation within smaller and larger groups (chapter 2); their sin (chapter 3); and their self-esteem (chapter 4). Such understanding is necessary because it is bound to apply both to counselors and counselees since they share a common humanity.

2

People

We have said already that the Bible gives no systematic account of human beings or their personalities, and that is abundantly true. It does, however, *refer* to human beings through the use of a number of different words and stories both in the Old Testament and the New Testament. The words are often connected, particularly in the Old Testament, with parts of the human body. Also, each word may have a number of different meanings and therefore may be translated in different ways. In spite of this, the words referring to human beings do convey a particular emphasis, especially when studied in light of the way individual biblical authors use them. Hence, while it is not possible to give accurate definitions of biblical person-words, we would be missing something valuable if we did not pay reasonable attention to the ways in which these words inform us. In the sections that follow, we shall trace the ways biblical person-words are used.

A. EXPLORATION WITHIN THE LAST CENTURY

For many centuries theologians had elaborated an account of human nature, dealing with such issues as the origin of human beings, their being made in the image and likeness of God, their freedom and destiny, their fall and sinfulness, and their redemption and re-creation in Christ. Then, shortly after the end of World War I, there occurred a new focus in the biblical way of describing human beings. This did not, of course, replace the earlier findings, but illuminated them. It was a shift from the more general to the more particular characteristics both of individual persons and corporate entities; and, furthermore, persons were to be studied within the dynamics of solidary life and relationships.

The fresh channel was created largely by the Danish scholar, Johannes Pedersen (e.g., in the volume: *Israel: Its Life and Culture*). What Pedersen did was to examine very carefully, within their contexts, the use in the Old Testament of a variety of person-words and group-words, and to spell out what they pointed to in our understanding of human beings. One result of his work was to shed new light on some traditional translations as given in the King James Version. Thus *nefesh*, for example, was unpacked to reveal something far removed from Plato's "soul" which had undoubtedly given a particular twist to the reader's earlier understanding.

Pedersen's work was followed by Aubrey Johnson's *The Vitality of the Individual in the Thought of Ancient Israel*, and H.W. Wolff's *Anthropology of the Old Testament*. As the twentieth century progressed and Old Testament studies developed further accuracy and sophistication, the view gained ground among biblical scholars that an individual person must be seen as a distinctive but unitary whole, rather than a partitioned one; and this issue will be discussed later.

As with Old Testament scholarship, so New Testament biblical scholars came to have an interest, during the twentieth century, in the meaning of person-words. Subsequently the connections between such words in the Old Testament and similar words in the New were of considerable interest. In some cases, the New can be equated almost completely with the Old. In other cases, however, there are certain differences of emphasis, and hence comparisons can be made only after careful consideration.

In the writings of Paul, for example, there is a striking flexibility with words. He may, indeed, address one word to a certain audience in a way which differs in emphasis from that used for another group. Once again he is likely to recruit a particular word to identify a theological concept or to become its symbol. In such case it has to be determined when he is using a word in a literal or bland sense, and when in a specialized or technical sense. Seminal contributions have been made to the study of Paul's person-words by writers such as Herman Ridderbos in *Paul: An Outline of His Theology* and by Robert Jewett, in *Paul's Anthropological Terms*; while W. Pannenberg's *Anthropology in Theological Perspective* has tackled the issues more inclusively than by reference solely to Paul.

B. "PERSONS" AND "FAMILIES" THROUGH OLD TESTAMENT EYES

There seems little doubt that certain words such as "flesh," "soul," "mind," and "spirit," in English translations of both Hebrew and Greek Scriptures, would be most aptly translated as "person" in many instances, and are so translated in some modern versions. In particular, the Hebrew *nefesh*, mentioned earlier, and the Greek *psyche* could well have "person" as a frequent rendering. Each of these can indicate a complete entity, as distinct from some part of an individual. We now explore relevant words from the Old Testament, acting as "pointers" rather than definitions, in an effort to build a biblical picture of people within their social context. We commence with an important group-word.

1. *Mishpaha*: solidarity and membership

Each human being is, first of all, to be seen *in solidarity* with other human beings as a member of a *mishpaha* or family. There are, of course, many kinds of "families," some being as inclusive as the nation, some as small as the immediate family; some contemporary, and some a grouping throughout time. Our membership within each is seen as a significant factor influencing who we are. "Solidarity" contains the insights, first, that what we are individually depends greatly on the groups to which we belong; and second, that we have an awareness of being one with a group, and in identification with it, especially in feeling and action. To quote Pedersen:

> Wherever those of one mind form a community round a common leader, they are a house *(mishpaha)*; and the leader who stamps it with his personality is its father, and those who join him are his sons [sic] . . . All living beings consist of this kind of unities, and the various characteristics and possibilities of every individual make him a part of many wholes.[1]

Mishpahoth (plural) could consist of closer or wider families, in which membership was scarcely voluntary. Or *mishpaha* could refer to "the sons of the prophets," where membership was voluntary; or it could be a family persisting over time, such as "the house of David," where the solidarity was in the tradition itself. There is the possibility, then, of a

---

1. Pedersen, *Israel: Its Life and Culture*, 54.

People

fellowship, communicated and shared, when people are together. The relationships within the *mishpaha* can, of course, be broken, and this is one manifestation of sin.

One of the practical things this tells us is that if we are interested in human beings, and with involvement in their development, we must be concerned first with understanding the relevant communities in which they already exist. Also, having attempted to capture the dynamics of an ideal community, we may envisage or possibly fashion such a community with those dynamics in view.

2. *Basar*: embodiment, communication, and relationship

Reinforcing the solidarity, sketched above, is the Hebrew notion of *basar* or "flesh." It is typical of Greek, and hence of modern Western thinking, to see the skin of a person as *dividing* him or her from another person. By contrast, Hebrew thought sees humankind as *unified* by the possession of flesh, as a substance that is common. Thus the elastic term *basar* refers basically to bodily substance (Genesis 2:21), but in the case of humans can be used to refer to the whole body (Proverbs 14:30), then to the whole personality (Psalm 16:9), then to the sexual union of a man and a woman (Genesis 2:24), then to the oneness of kinship (2 Samuel 19:12,13), and finally to the totality of human existence (Job 34:14,15). So much for embodiment.

In addition, however, communication and relationship can also be associated with *basar*. Yahweh declares: "My Spirit will not contend with human beings forever, for they are *basar*" (Genesis 6:3). The Psalmist says, with great feeling: "my heart and my *basar* cry out for the living God" (Psalm 84:2b). And Ezekiel promises: "I will give them an undivided heart and put a new spirit in them; I will remove from them their heart of stone and give them a heart of *basar*" (Ezekiel 11:19).

It is worthwhile, in passing, to note the dignity inhering, biblically, in *basar*. Humans were created capable of providing a body for the Word of God, and God the Word spoke, not only through words, but through living genuinely within the commonness of our body substance.

3. *Nefesh*: distinctiveness, organization, agency, and fulfillment

As has already been said, *nefesh* can refer to a human being in totality, e.g., Psalm 23:3, but in addition, a totality *with a peculiar stamp*, e.g., Job 16:4, where a literal translation would be, "if *your nefesh* were in the place of *my nefesh*." This distinctiveness, discernible in the whole person, is sometimes to be seen as an influence permeating all its parts and sometimes as the central core of the person. So, with this in mind, *nefesh* would seem rather close to some twentieth-century ideas of "*personality.*" (In the following assertions of Pedersen and others, the references or comments in square brackets are by this writer and are intended as partial, but by no means complete, indicators of the point being made. To assemble all the biblical evidence would be too large a task to tackle here, and consequently the reader is referred to the original publications in order to appreciate the cogency of any conclusion.)

We draw attention, now, to Pedersen's slant on the *organizational* aspect of *nefesh*:

> The best characterisation of the soul [*nefesh*] is as an organism, which at any time centres and ranges itself round a point of gravity [e.g., Psalm 10:3,4 where the rival points of gravity are "cravings" or "Yahweh"]. This point is the centre of force in which action is created [e.g., Genesis 2:7] and the centre must be firm and strong [e.g., Judges 5:21b and Leviticus 5:1, emphasizing responsibility]; otherwise the soul must not be stiff but pliable, so that it subordinates itself to its centre[Isaiah 26:8,9a].[2]

In psychological terms, this would seem to suggest the organization, or integration, or dovetailing of the various aspects of personal functioning around some clear commitment. In counseling terms, it would, on the one hand, distinguish between the kind of person who held ethical principles centrally and strongly, but was also able to discern sensitively the various applications of such to everyday life; and, on the other, the kind of person who organized life according to hard-and-fast rules of action, without reference back to central principles.

Further from Pedersen, this time on *agency* and a resulting *interaction* between persons:

> A human being cannot be isolated, as this is contrary to its disposition. It must act, i.e., act on others . . .
> [e.g., 1 Chronicles 22:19, where "seeking Yahweh" is spelt out in terms of *the actions* of "building the sanctuary" and "bringing the ark into the temple "]

---

2. Ibid., 145.

> ... and itself be acted upon by others; in that manner the souls are brought into real contact with each other ...
> [e.g., 1 Samuel 25:29, where Abigail declares that the *nefesh* of David will be *bound securely in the bundle of the living*.]
> ... This openness towards other souls, or this pliability, is part of the fundamental character of the soul, and for that the soul is created.[3]

Mutual openness and mutual agency of persons are factors making for growth in personal relationships and also for the emergence of person-to-person ethics (e.g., Genesis 9:5). The involvement of agency is, in itself, highly significant. Human beings are basically active, rather than purely responsive beings in the manner of "zombies."

While factors such as agency contribute "shape" to the person, nevertheless the *nefesh* is not to be viewed exclusively in an architectural way. The person is also *capable of a rich quality of experience*. Once again Pedersen breaks into the concept, and emerges with the following idiomatic and intuitive depiction:

> It is the nature of the soul to be full and happy ... when the soul is filled, it grows, expands ... that ... is the happiness of the soul: to be filled, to thrive, to expand ... [e.g., Psalm 63:5 and Proverbs 16:24]
> ... as the happy soul is wide, so the anguished soul is narrow ... the anguished soul is *empty*.[4] [e.g., Job 30:11,15,16, ending with "And now my *nefesh* ebbs away."]

Enrichment, growth, and an accompanying satisfaction are thus considered possible and indeed normal for the person.

4. *Ruach* and *leb*: orientation and central core

This is the point in our discussion where it becomes useful to arm ourselves with a long-standing threefold description applying to human experience. For those from ancient times, and right through to the present, it has been useful to think of the following categories: the cognitive, the affective, and the active or behavioral, the last of these having formerly been called "the conative." The cognitive deals with the area of thought, knowledge, reflection, and reasoning—the functions now attributed to the left brain.

3. Ibid., 165.
4. Ibid., 148–9.

Walking Alongside

The affective is a technical term covering everything from mild feelings to extreme emotions. The active or behavioral is more self-explanatory, and refers to human involvements which commence with intention, continue through motivation, and conclude with action. We do not claim any fundamental status for this threefold description of human experience, but we do claim that it is quite useful to think in these terms, particularly while examining imprecise biblical person-words.

Leb and *ruach* are alike in that both present a view of the person as *oriented*. With these two Hebrew words in mind, it would be a truism to say, "a person is where he or she faces," or to expand this a little: "a person is significantly formed through the focus of his or her life." (For *ruach*, see Psalm 31:1–5, ending, "Into your hands I commit my *ruach*; redeem me, Yahweh, my faithful God." For *leb*, see 1 Kings 14:8,9.)

Looking at the same things from a slightly different angle: whatever it is that the person centers upon is his or her object of worship and, in this context, each of *nefesh, leb,* and *ruach* can refer to *the core or the center of one's being,* such *soul, heart,* or *spirit* being understood as directional, oriented, worshipful. So far as *heart* is concerned, see 1 Kings 11:4 where we are told:

> As Solomon grew old, his wives turned his *leb* after other gods, and his *leb* was not fully devoted to Yahweh[5] his God, as the *leb* of David his father had been. He followed Ashtoreth the goddess of the Sidonians, and Molek the detestable god of the Ammonites.

In Psalm 77:6, Asaph recorded: "My *leb* meditated and my *ruach* asked." And Isaiah, through poetic parallelism, uses *nefesh* and *ruach* as virtually synonymous when he confides:

> My *soul* yearns for you in the night;
> in the morning my *spirit* longs for you.[6]

A further likeness is that both *leb* and *ruach* incorporate a balance in the threefold facets of functioning—thinking, feeling, and doing—rather than being restricted to one. Some scholars have claimed that *leb* carries, in spite of its usual translation "heart," rather more of a cognitive emphasis, usually conveyed in English by "mind," and that *ruach*, in contrast, carries rather more of an affective emphasis. What is clear is that both

---

5. I have used "Yahweh" as the alternative for the TNIV's "the Lord."
6. Isaiah 26:9

imply all of thinking, feeling, and doing within their scope, even though their emphases may differ.

Ruach, already mentioned, now requires a little further attention. It is breath, or wind, or spirit. It tends to be a call-and-answer, or a move-and-respond connection between God as Spirit and a human being as spirit, indicating a potential communion between these two breath-beings. The person, as *ruach*, has the ability to communicate with God, and also the capacity for receiving communications from him, resulting in personal change (see especially Psalm 51:10–12).

5. Persons: a summary of perspectives from the Old Testament

- *The person is nefesh*: a needy human being, firmly rooted in the created order, whose nature is to act with respect to God and other humans, and to be acted upon by them.
- *The person is basar*: a flesh-being who, as such, shares physical commonness and psychic unity with others, and is geared for fellowship and communication with them.
- *The person is leb*: a being who functions thoughtfully, feelingly, and purposefully.
- *The person is ruach*: a breath-being, subject to being moved, particularly towards God.
- *The person is nefesh-leb-ruach*: an oriented being, or the central core of such a being.
- *The person lives within mishpahoth*: a being socially shaped and socially related.

C. "PERSONS" AND "CHURCHES" THROUGH NEW TESTAMENT EYES

1. *Ekklesia*

As in the case of the Old Testament, we look first at a highly important *group* word—in this case *ekklesia*. Once again, the human being is seen in solidarity with others, but this is particularly highlighted in connection with the gathering of Christian believers. *Ekklesiai* are groups for whom physical meeting of a voluntary kind along with the spontaneous personal communication which is normal within them are central features (Acts 12:1–17). They are characterized by interdependence, not only in the sense that each member is supported and built up by the gifts of others, but also in the sense that an individual member contributes to the atmosphere and functioning of the total group, while the ethos and pattern of relationships of the total group contribute simultaneously to the individual (Ephesians 2:11—4:16).

While the recognition of this interdependence renders impossible any sharp demarcation between individual and group, nevertheless it is possible to talk sensibly about qualities which apply both at the individual and the group levels.

One such quality is "maturity," the notion which will be discussed in section E of this chapter. The New Testament *ekklesiai* were smallish gatherings with an average size of about thirty. Such a size encouraged the growth of committed personal relationships among those who came regularly; and undoubtedly facilitated by this, Paul's most significant metaphor for these groups was that of *a particular kind of family* (1 Cor 4:6–16), although he also spelled out another metaphor of the church group as *a functioning human body* (1 Cor 10:16,17,32).

2. *Psyche*

Just as *nefesh* refers to a human being in a rather general way, *psyche* does similarly, and with many of the same connotations. It ranges in meaning from the sharp focus of "an individual" (Matthew 10:39), to a much more general meaning such as "life" or "a life" (Matthew 6:25–27). But, as mentioned earlier, in some cases it would simply be translated as "person" (e.g., 1 Peter 3:20b).

3. *Nous* and *kardia*

Nous comes, in much classical Greek, with a strong intellectual, or rational, or cognitive force. An important question immediately arises, particularly in the Pauline letters: does Paul, in his *koine* Greek, use this in the traditional sense, or does he modify and bend it within his theological model?

According to Ridderbos, we must answer by affirming the latter alternative.[7] Seen in this light, *nous* encompasses not only the grasping or understanding of the message that has been received, chiefly a cognitive process, but also the personal response to it, at least in part, affective; and, as well, the action taken in the world of persons and things, and hence practical or behavioral (e.g., Romans 1:28). Thus *nous*, while including the classical meaning as an element, now refers to a total coordinated response of the person and therefore, by implication, to a fully functioning person.

Kardia seems to function in Paul's writings in a way scarcely distinguishable from *nous*, so that Ridderbos and others refer for convenience to *nous-kardia* as essentially the one concept. If any distinction is to be made, Ridderbos finds that the cognitive or rational does tend to be somewhat more pronounced in *nous* and the affective in *kardia*, but reminds us that all three strands, inclusive of the behavioral—and within this, especially moral action—occur in both. Hence a fairly good colloquial English translation of either *nous* or *kardia* would be "heart and mind." And, as with *leb* and *ruach*, the intention is often to refer to the center of one's being, when focused or worshipful.

This holistic rendering of *nous* is pointedly illustrated by the well-known passage from Paul's letter to the Romans, chapter 12, verse 2:

> Do not conform to the pattern of this world, but be transformed by the renewing of your *mind*.

Virtually all translations, as in the TNIV quoted here, render *nous* by the word "mind." A great deal depends, of course, on a contemporary understanding of the word "mind" in English. Its meaning is, and has been over the centuries, rather imprecise, and usually dependent on the philosophical theory lying behind it. It is instructive, from one angle, that the *Contemporary English Version* translates verse 2 as follows:

> Don't be like the people of this world, but let God change *the way you think*.

Here obviously, is a clearly cognitive emphasis in line with classical Greek.

The translation which comes nearest to conveying what Ridderbos has in mind is that by Arthur Way in *The Letters of Saint Paul*. He translates thus:

> Do not conform to the externalities of this world; nay, let your characters be transformed by the birth of *a new life purpose*.

---

7. *Paul: An Outline of His Theology*, 118–9.

Having a life purpose involves rather more than thinking, or reasoning, or learning and gets a little closer to the totality of the person's experience. The kind of translation we would have in view would, unfortunately, be rather pedantic, thus:

> ... be being transformed by the ongoing renewing of *your affections, your thinking, and your actions.*

Whatever the translation, however, an exclusively cognitive interpretation places an over-emphasis on the believer's thinking processes and tends to imply, along with some of the Stoics and Albert Ellis in the nineteenth century, that significant transformation *originates* in a change of thought. When shifted across into counseling theory, the holistic interpretation spells out implications in a markedly different way from the one which gives temporal precedence to the cognitive.

In this connection it seems timely to refer to the work of Joel B. Green who has skillfully related the findings of biblical anthropology to a sophisticated understanding of recent advances in neuroscience. Relevant to the above discussion of the Pauline use of *nous*, Green declares:

> As we have seen, the most basic and significant contribution of cognitive science is its irreducible emphasis on somatic existence as the basis and means of human existence, including the exercise of the mind. From this we might infer, for example, *the fallacy of imagining that intellect and affect are separable, the fallacy of imagining that mind and behavior are separable, the fallacy of imagining that human life can be understood merely or primarily with respect to individuals, and the inescapable conclusion that human formation is a process.* In important ways, *these emphases correlate with NT perspectives* on Christian conversion, so crucial to its depiction of the new humanity called forth in Christ.[8]

4. *Pneuma*

There seems to be a considerable parallel between *ruach* and *pneuma*, so much so that the suggestion of communication and communion between God and the believer, noted in the understanding of *ruach*, appears to be made quite explicit in what Paul says about "spirit." Thus we see, especially

---

8. Green, *Body, Soul, and Human Life*, 122. Emphases added.

in Romans 8:16, the affirmation: "The Spirit himself testifies with our spirit that we are God's children."

Frequently, however, rather than using the notion of *pneuma* to represent the person, Paul chooses to speak of the believer being *in the Spirit* (e.g., 2 Corinthians 6:6), walking or living *by the Spirit* (e.g., Galatians 5:16), keeping *in step with the Spirit* (e.g., Galatians 5:25), or being a person *filled with the Spirit* (e.g., Ephesians 5:18).

5. *Sarx* and *Pneuma*

The literal translation of *sarx* is "flesh." And it can be noted that Paul uses *sarx* at times in this normal and neutral way (e.g., 2 Corinthians 12:7). This is similar to some of the ways in which *basar* is used, though it is not as likely to carry the same communicative overtones.

In addition, however, he uses *sarx* in a quite technical sense, when he opposes it—translated as "the sinful nature"—to the orientation of the Spirit *(pneuma)* especially in Romans 7 and Galatians 5. In this context, *sarx* stands for any orientation opposed to God, whatever form that might take; and whether or not it is geared more to sexual, intellectual, aesthetic, pragmatic, or other practices.

6. *Soma*

Soma, literally "body," is frequently used by Paul to refer to "the church"—the corporate body. There is, however, an individual use which comes very close in meaning to the present-day term "personality." This individual use of *soma* was brought to light by J.A.T. Robinson in his book *The Body*. The words of Jesus about "the whole body" being in one case, full of darkness, but in the other, full of light, head in a similar direction, even though authored by Matthew rather than Paul.

Extracting the basic message from the context of 1 Corinthians 6:13b–16, which passage is wrestling with foods, stomachs, and sexual immorality, the quite general and startling statement is: "The body . . . is . . . meant . . . for the Lord, and the Lord for the body." This is followed by the declaration: "Whoever is united with the Lord is one with him in spirit."

The personality, then, flourishes within its intended home, through union with Christ, being associated, in Paul's mind, with both *soma* and *pneuma*.

Walking Alongside

As in the previous section, it is time to summarize our exploration of people or persons, seen through the writers of the New Testament, especially Paul. However, it seems sensible, in addition, to do this through comparisons with the person-words already described in the discussion of the Old Testament.

7. People or persons: a brief summary of perspectives from the New Testament

- *The person is psyche*: its meaning rather similar to *nefesh*.
- *The person is pneuma*: its meaning very similar to *ruach*.
- *The person is nous*: its meaning holistic and somewhat like *leb*.
- *The person is nous-kardia*: indicating, as with *leb-ruach,* the core of one's being, or the stance of being oriented.
- *The person is either sarx* or *pneuma*, according to the direction of orientation: towards anything other than God, or towards God himself.
- *The person is soma*: the being for whom integration and focus can occur through a close relationship with God.
- *The believing person lives within ekklesiai,* local and heavenly, which affect personal shape and relationships, and have some elements in common with *mishpahoth*.

D. PEOPLE: JIGSAWS OR JEWELS?

1. Parts or wholes?

Though previous sections of this chapter have concentrated on biblical person-pointers from the Old and New Testaments respectively, the summary, given immediately above, has begun the process of viewing persons from an overall biblical stance. This section will pursue a similarly inclusive approach.

Certain theologians, when confronted by biblical person-words such as "body," "soul," and "spirit," have been inclined to see these as *parts* of the whole comprising the person. And this tendency has been linked, at times, with the philosophical views of Platonists, who envisaged an immaterial inner identity surrounded or even confined by an external and material bodily existence. This kind of view has been described as a "ghost in the machine."

However, it is not so much this, or any other particular theory, that entranced such theologians, but rather the intellectual habit of seeing humans as consisting of parts: in other words, a *jigsaw*, and this view has been bequeathed by centuries of reflection. It is, indeed, an extremely difficult task to describe wholes without invoking a jigsaw model. Once the complex whole, such as a person, has been analyzed or reduced to component parts, there are very great difficulties involved—as in the precedent of Humpty Dumpty—in putting these together again into an interconnected and functioning unit. It is interesting that the "person-as-parts" biblical position produced its own internal controversy, in that some saw the person as *tripartite*, a threesome, while others saw the person as *bipartite*, a twosome.

We now look at some passages of Scripture on this issue.

(a) In Deuteronomy 6:4–5, Moses declares:

> Hear, O Israel: The LORD our God, the LORD is one. Love the LORD your God with all your heart *[lebab]* and with all your soul *[nefesh]* and with all your strength *[me'od]*,

the last word being more adverbial in force, and meaning "greatly" or "very much." Would this, then, be *bipartite*, with an adverb attached for emphasis?

Mark's quotation of the very same passage from the Septuagint (Mark 12:30) is:

> with all your heart *[kardia]* and with all your soul *[psyche]* and with all your mind *[dianora]* and with all your strength *[ischys or "greatly"]*

Would this be *tripartite*, "mind" having being added, as well as an adverb?

(b) In 1 Thessalonians 5:23b Paul refers, in a passage strongly relied upon by the tripartite school, to: "your whole spirit *[pneuma]*, soul *[psyche]* and body *[soma]*."

Though, like the passage in Mark, this could be called *tripartite*, two of the ingredients differ from those in Mark.

(c) In Matthew 10:28, we have a reference merely to *soma* and *psyche*. Is this *bipartite*?

(d) In Matthew 6:22, it is sufficient for Jesus to say: "If your eyes are healthy, your whole body will be full of light."

Is this, then, *monopartite*?

2. A new figure of speech

In contrast to the above analytic approach, what we are frequently faced with, in both Testaments, is the piling up or accumulation of terms, each of which can refer to a whole person, but each with a certain slant or perspective on that person. Just as a *simile* is a likeness between two things, and a *metaphor* is a figurative identity between two things, so we shall call this heaping up of terms, where each refers to the same object or person, a *cumulus*, which adds a sense of wholeness and completeness. Rather than conveying an analysis, it brings an impression of synthesis.

This model, which is preferred to the one viewing people as parts, sees them as *jewels*—in a sense precious, yes, but not necessarily beautiful! They are not jewels which present a determinate number of facets, as is often the case with diamonds, for this would reinforce the jigsaw model: a part refracting green light, a part red light, and so on. Let us imagine that they form a whole, perhaps spherical, which can be surveyed from many angles, yielding multiple perspectives.

E. PEOPLE: MATURE OR UNDERDEVELOPED?

1. Health, normality, and maturity

In our earlier discussion of "counsel," we included two related processes: on the one hand, *building* the resources of people towards, and on the other hand, *restoring* people to *a normal or acceptable state of wellbeing*. Included were both personal change and therapy. Of course, what is "normal" or "acceptable" varies according to one's world view and, as an aspect of that, to one's view of persons functioning within their community. This chapter has been attempting to spell out a biblical view drawn from both Old and New Testaments.

The question now arises whether there exists a down-to-earth goal, within Christian experience, which will both incorporate standards and give some indication, as well, how one is progressing towards their achievement. Such a norm is to be found in Paul's idea of *maturity*. As we observed with the notion of *counseling*, the biblical idea may not be identical with the way the word is understood in contemporary English, but the overlap is sufficient for us to apply the crux of the biblical term to our modern practice. Bearing this in mind, Paul's idea of *maturity* overlaps sufficiently with the current notion of *health,* to be able to contribute to it a biblical understanding.

I have argued elsewhere[9] that health of personality refers to an ideal state of affairs within the sphere of personality, judged by the efficiency of its performance in coping with the conditions bearing upon, and necessary for, such performance. While secular psychologists have worked with a view similar to or identical with this, the relevant conditions have, understandably, included only such factors as human traits and relationships, in addition to medical, social, and cultural influences. And such an approach has proved theoretically and practically useful. But it does not include relationships existing among God, human beings, their societies, and their cultures; and these conditions, explored throughout the Bible, can be expected to bring significant differences into our conception of wellbeing or health.

2. Adulthood: a Pauline perspective

> When I was a child, my speech, my outlook and my thoughts were all childish. When I grew up, I had finished with childish things (1 Corinthians 13:11, New English Bible).

Paul's letters are "shot through" with the conviction that it is important for Christians to "grow up," i.e., to be moving towards adulthood. He is joined in this assertion by other New Testament writers such as the author of Hebrews (e.g., 5:11—6:2). While Jesus extolled the humble or helpless status of the child, and saw it as exemplary in *coming to faith,* Paul's focus was upon the need for *growth within faith.* To remain a child in the latter context would be spiritually pitiable. Adulthood, or maturity, therefore features as an ideal for Christian development.

In modern speech "mature" can be a very slippery word, devoid of precise meaning and referring to anyone we happen to approve of. Paul's word is *teleios.* We need to examine it carefully to grasp the contours of its meaning. But first, a linguistic story, as a way in.

Some years ago my family and I were sharing a house at a student conference with a renowned classical scholar and his family. Both of us were giving a series of addresses to a large, young, and—on the whole!—appreciative audience. I asked him what was the meaning of *teleios.* His

---

9. Andersen, *Health of Personality.*

immediate reply was "one who has achieved his or her goals." This taught me one thing, but caused me to question another.

I was taught that *teleios* was cognate with *telos*—a goal or end-point—and I shall return shortly to this important "find." What I questioned, however, was how *teleios* could possibly mean "an achiever" in the context of Philippians 3:12–13, where Paul protests:

> Not that I have already obtained all this, or have already arrived at my goal *[teteleiomai]*;
> and
> Brothers and sisters, *I do not consider myself yet to have taken hold of it.*[emphases added]

My colleague was gracious enough to agree that, while Paul sometimes retained the "completion" or "perfection" notion of *teleios* and cognates in the manner of classical Greek, he obviously used it to convey a quite different meaning—*maturity*—in the Philippians passage we had been considering. We now consider some of the ingredients of this important Christian idea.

3. Goal-pursuit

Taking up the hint that the *teleios* or mature person is somehow connected with having goals, a great deal of light was now thrown on the third chapter of the Philippian Letter, in that it overflows with goals:

> I consider everything a loss because of *the surpassing worth of knowing Christ Jesus* my Lord, for whose sake I have lost all things. I consider them garbage, *that I may gain Christ, and be found in him* . . . *I want to know Christ*—yes, to know the power of his resurrection and participation in his suffering . . . and so, somehow, attaining to the resurrection from the dead (Philippians 3:8–11; emphases added).

The total impression given here is of a person desiring the goal, above all, of *a personal and intimate relationship with his Lord,* knowing that this will involve identification with him, along with all that this implies in terms of action. While specifically denying that he had "arrived" or was perfect, Paul continues to spell out the situation saying:

> *I press on to take hold of that for which Christ Jesus took hold of me*
> . . .

> Forgetting what is behind and straining toward what is ahead, *I press on toward the goal* . . . (3:12–14)
> All of us, then, who are *mature* should take such a view of things (3:15; emphases added).

His maturity is displayed, not in a state of placid contemplation, *but in an all-out present pursuit of his great but specific goals*, making his own that purpose for the achievement of which Christ had made Paul *his own*.

The person who is mature is not, then, the one who has achieved all of his or her basic goals, but the one who has them clearly in mind and is pursuing them vigorously. In addition, Paul is aware that he is merely contributing to the already-moving and ever-flowing current of God's purposes. And so, throughout the account, and in spite of the fact that in nine verses Paul has used "I" eleven times, one nevertheless gains the impression of humility, gratitude, and partnership. His acute self-awareness does not compromise his zest for knowing God and being identified with Christ. On the contrary, it would seem to have been necessary, in order to express fully his personal alignment.

4. Suffering: a sobering complication

In chapter 1, the confronting questions were raised whether distress should always be alleviated, and also whether distress or suffering is not at times a very good teacher. The following remarks are not intended to be a response to the philosophical issue of "why pain"? They are, however, intended to display the relevance of suffering *within Paul's notion of maturity*. Furthermore, Paul's angle on suffering will certainly have appropriate applications to the situation of many a client in the early years of the twenty-first century.

The fact is that the dedicated pursuit of goals, identified earlier as an indicator of maturity, is not necessarily always a "happy" experience. There will be many occasions when the atmosphere of the Olympics, noted in Philippians 3:13–14, may be markedly absent. Romans 5:1–5 brings the insight that "pressing on" may not involve us in adrenalin-packed restructuring of thought, emotion, and planning; but may, in fact, be cashed out through "struggling on." The latter could well be called "resilience," provided only that it is distinguished from other current uses of the term.

Those who are committed unreservedly to the pursuit of Christian goals will, from time to time, find the more obvious paths blocked and feel frustration rising within themselves. The alternatives would seem to be either resting content with a postponement of action until the present blockage has been removed, or discovering new means of pressing towards the same goal. The fact that endurance means not merely frustration but also an opportunity for growth, will point to the futility of mere activism, the confidence that clever or forceful action will achieve our goals. The Romans passage, then, not only gives balance to the goal-seeking mood of the Philippians Letter, but also suggests a Spirit-response in situations where "straining forward" and "pressing on" are thwarted.

Having faced this reality, however, there is another side to the situation which must be brought into view. With the hope of sharing the glory of God as our goal,

> we also glory in our sufferings, because we know that suffering produces perseverance; perseverance, character; and character, hope. And hope does not put us to shame (Romans 5:2–5).

Here Paul is once again pressing his theme of development towards adulthood, though here he does not supply the name "maturity." In a passage which is remarkably similar, however, James declares (1:2–4) that facing trials should be considered *pure joy*, because

> the testing of your faith produces perseverance. Let perseverance finish its work so that you may be mature *[teleios]* and complete, not lacking anything.

Switching back now to Paul's developmental series, it is interesting that in the sequence suffering . . . endurance . . . character, the character mentioned is what has been developed when the believer is put to the test, and then found to be "tried," "true," or "fit": the crucible out of which "hope" may emerge. The process is, then, that by means of suffering, endurance, or perseverance, proven or mature character will emerge. It is all-of-a-piece with the goal, in Philippians, of wanting to share Christ's sufferings. The rejoicing (Paul) or the pure joy (James) is a fulfillment or a satisfaction rather than a hedonistic response; and believers are themselves seriously modified when they have experienced it. The differences between "happiness" and "fulfillment" are explored later, at some depth, in chapter 8.

5. Maturity: a corporate achievement

Thus far in our plunge into Paul's maturity model, we have focused only upon Paul's individual experience and behavior, and, in parallel, that of individual believers. As in our treatment of person-words, however, we need to acknowledge simultaneously the solidary or corporate element in his idea of adulthood. The fourth chapter of the Ephesian Letter contributes this perspective in short compass, but yet in considerable detail. Indeed, what we have in Ephesians 4:2–16 is a remarkable statement of the interdependence of individual and group.

For a start, the passage is notable for its use of phrases suggestive of maturity: "so that the body . . . may be built up," " become mature," "attaining to the whole measure of the fullness of Christ," " no longer be infants," " in all things grow up," " grows and builds itself up in love," and " growing up into . . . Christ." It claims that special Christians, acting as "gifts" within their respective roles, contribute to the building up of the corporate body, the church, and its work of ministry, with the result that God's people, the individuals involved, mature (4:11–14). Similarly these people, when "speaking the truth in love" continue to grow into Christ, thus contributing to the life of the whole body which itself grows and is built up (4: 15,16).

Thus the growth and final maturity of the individual Christian contribute to the growth and final maturity of the church, the organism of which he or she is a member. Conversely, the growth and maturity of the church are a significant influence in the growth and maturity of the individuals involved. The Christian individual and the Christian group, therefore, through their mutual entwinement around, or attachment to Christ, are interdependent. This is an example, in the theological realm, of the circular process which has become well known to students of social phenomena.

6. Love: the integrating glue

From Ephesians 4:16, a further issue emerges. A dynamic affecting both group and individual is spelled out:

> From him the whole body, joined and held together by every supporting ligament, grows and builds itself up in *love [agape]* as each part does its work. (emphasis added)

Link this with a further statement from the Colossian Letter, probably written at much the same time as Ephesians, where Paul is counseling his readers to put on compassion, kindness, humility, gentleness, and patience, and we shall discover an extension of this theme.

> And over all these virtues put on *love, which binds them all together* in perfect unity (Colossians 3:14; emphasis added).

Thus the new characteristics of the new nature are held together, forged into a unity, integrated by *agape*. Once again the same thought is expressed where Paul prays that his readers, being

> *rooted and established in love,* may have power . . . to grasp how wide and long and high and deep is the love of Christ, and to know this love (Ephesians 3:17–19; emphasis added).

Here the exploration of the vast dimensions of Christian experience is made possible because the believer is surrounded, nourished, and developed by an ethos of loving relationship and activity. A true Christian solidarity is unimaginable without the unifying surround of *agape*, its atmosphere, and its action. A fuller treatment of love is given later in chapter 7.

7. Maturity in ethical judgments

We noted earlier in this chapter that the writer to the Hebrews appeared to share Paul's understanding of the mature person. In chapter 5 of that letter a distinction is made between "milk," appropriate for infants and "solid food," appropriate for the mature, the adults. Infants in the faith have to be taught the elementary truths of God's word from the beginning. Solid food, which includes teaching about righteousness, is the diet for the mature,

> who by constant use have trained themselves to distinguish good from evil (Hebrews 5:14).

Paul, when dealing with the issue of wisdom in 1 Corinthians, claims to speak a message of wisdom *among the mature*. He continues by saying that God's secret wisdom has been revealed by his Spirit, and that we have received the Spirit so that we may understand what God has freely given us. His rather startling conclusion is that "the Spirit-person"—obviously identical, in view of his treatment, with "the mature person"—makes judgments about all things, and has the mind of Christ! Such judgments will cover many areas but, as the writer to the Hebrews insists, will feature *ethical judgments*: matters of right and wrong.

A contemporary philosopher, John Kleinig, in a perceptive essay supplies a useful link between the possibility of moral action and the stature of the person involved.

> It is a characteristic of human beings, or at least of those who have reached a certain level of maturity, that they are not simply the meeting points of external forces, but possess a capacity to stand back from or transcend the various forces which press in upon them, and to choose which path they will follow. It is in that capacity that the possibility of morality resides.[10]

While not denying this possibility to human beings in general, both Paul and the writer to the Hebrews are emphasizing the quickening and the empowerment, in ethical matters, that the Spirit brings within believers who are becoming adult in the course of their Christian journey.

8. Summary

Maturity, in the writings of Paul and several other New Testament authors, means being adult or fully grown, having basic Christian goals in mind, and pursuing them vigorously. This pursuit may well encounter a variety of adverse experiences which introduce suffering and frustration. Out of these, however, can emerge character which is tried, tested, and mature.

But the path to maturity is not solely an individual matter. It is true that the gifts of individual Christians and their maturity contribute to the efficiency and maturity of the church, or other Christian group, but the reverse is also true: the two are complementary. Love is the supreme person-builder and acts to unify all aspects of Christian character. "Spirit-persons," i.e., mature Christians, become equipped, in the process of growth, to make sound judgments on all significant questions, and in particular, on questions of ethics.

F. THE NATURE OF PERSONS IN BIBLICAL PERSPECTIVE

The central thrust of this book is that there are some basic theological presuppositions that it would be natural for a biblical Christian engaged in counseling to bring, consciously or unconsciously, to his or her work. The area dealt with in this chapter has been *a biblical understanding of people*.

10. Kleinig, "Moral education and the nature of morality," 32.

Walking Alongside

What we have in mind here is not a collection of personal or cultural traits, as in a compendium; nor a survey of mental health deficiencies, as in the DSM,[11] nor, conversely, a listing of character strengths. The intention has been to convey an overall scriptural perspective on human beings active within their communities. Largely this points to the potentialities they have, due to their creation by God. It also includes, as an integral part, the possibility of receiving messages from God and responding to these. One issue related to all aspects of this, is *the nature of sin*, along with the changes this brings to human personality and action. This is dealt with next, in a separate chapter, not only because of its inherent importance, but also because it is so little recognized in the literature of psychology or counseling.

Within the scope of theology, we have been exploring the area of biblical or theological anthropology, i.e., the study of persons, their societies, and cultures. As in any branch of theology, questions of interpretation arise, known technically as hermeneutics. What this implies is that the findings of this chapter, and indeed of the whole book, may well be challenged, even by those who, like the present writer, share the conviction expressed in 2 Timothy 3:16,

> All Scripture is God-breathed and is useful for teaching, rebuking, correcting and training in righteousness, so that all God's people may be thoroughly equipped for every good work.

Hopefully, however, challenges will be matters of detail. In any case, the overall message is that the Bible says plenty about human beings, and that if these things are not already part of the mindset of the counselor who is Christian, such a person might be willing to make their acquaintance! *Some* of the insights that follow are built into *some* current approaches to counseling. Those involving communication and relationship with God do not find resonance with any secular approaches. There is a need, then, for Christians engaged in counseling to subject the models of counseling, currently in use, to a process of sifting through the mesh provided by scriptural criteria. There follows now a summary of what has been discussed in detail in the course of the chapter.

---

11. i.e., Diagnostic and Statistical Manual of Mental Disorders.

CONCLUSION AND TRANSITION

People are perceived in the Bible as wholes, but from differing vantage points which are listed below.

1. The person: a participant entity
The person is seen here as a member of groups, either voluntarily or inescapably; emerging with *a social shape* that accommodates the requirements and ethos of such groups by mutual reinforcement or mutual compromise; and that also yields the possibility of fellowship with other participants.

2. The person: a distinctive entity
The person is seen still as a functioning whole but, to repeat Pedersen's phrase, a totality *with a peculiar stamp*. Many, in our day, affirm this insight, either psychologically, arising from wide clinical experience; or biologically, with evidence drawn from the distinctiveness demonstrated by DNA readings.

3. The person: a communications system
The person is seen as a sender and receiver of messages; and one who may relate warmly to others similarly equipped. Awareness of *a shared humanity* is built into this perspective, and is indeed a protection against the idea of a human being as highly individualistic. An extension of this will be seen in 8, below.

4. The person: a focused entity
The person is here seen in terms of how he or she is *orientated*; and flowing from this, in describing the *life-focus which has been embraced*. In theological terms, the person is seen in the light of his or her center of worship: the nucleus around which life and personality revolve.

5. The person: equipped to become Spirit-related
The person is seen here in terms of *responsiveness to the overtures of God the Spirit, along with a humble assertiveness* in prayer through the same Spirit. The term "spiritual" has been avoided, because its vague and comprehensive use, in current speech, lacks the precision needed for the intimate link between God and a person.

6. The person: an integrated entity
The person is seen here first, in terms of *the strengths of core beliefs and values* which ground his or her identity; and secondly in terms of the way that *diverse thoughts, feelings, actions, and interpretations may*, over time, *be appropriately included* within the core.

7. The person: a fulfilled entity
The person is here seen as being *enriched and satisfied in the process of growth towards God-likeness*; as opposed to being devoted to the trivial, and being empty of personal or social significance.

8. The person: a relational entity
The person is seen as one who, in the process of acting upon others and being acted upon by them, may develop *access to the inner personal experience of those others*, through mutual openness and agency, and through growth in personal relationship. The person may experience this *access both to God and to fellow humans*.

9. The person: a developing entity
The person is seen as one growing from "babyhood" to "adulthood" ideally through identification with Christ, through the vigorous pursuit of goals, through suffering, and through the giving and receiving of love within a sharing Christian community. With this maturing comes a unifying process within personal character, and a growing ability to make sound judgments.

All of the above has been presented in what might be called an ideal form. It is as though "God saw all that he had made [and especially male and female human beings] and it was very good" (Genesis 1: 27, 31). However, from Genesis 2 and onwards throughout Scripture, we are faced with a penetration of evil, which is called *sin*, and which distorts the shape, and inhibits the growth, individually and communally, of otherwise beautiful beings. We examine this reality in the following chapter.

3

Sin

> The webbing together of God, humans, and all creation in justice, fulfillment, and delight is what the Hebrew prophets called *shalom*. We call it peace, but it means far more than mere peace of mind or a cease-fire between enemies. In the Bible, shalom means *universal flourishing, wholeness, and delight*—a rich state of affairs in which natural needs are satisfied and natural gifts fruitfully employed, a state of affairs that inspires joyful wonder as its Creator and Savior opens doors and welcomes the creatures in whom he delights. *Shalom,* in other words, *is the way things ought to be.*[1]

Manifestly Cornelius Plantinga has chosen to commence his Breviary by spelling out *an ideal* which encompasses the relationships among God, human beings, and the creation. The advantage lies in glimpsing, first, the spiritual and moral beauty of such relationships, before being confronted with their absence or distortion. To look fully and broadly at divine intention is then to have the horror of pollution and attempted destruction brought into stark relief.

---

1. Plantinga, *Not the Way It's Supposed To Be,* 10. (Emphasis in the last sentence is mine.)

A. HOW DISTURBING!

It is, then, against the backdrop of God's *creative and redemptive ways* of dealing with his creation that sin will be discerned as powerful, certainly, but also *parasitic*. It features as the Opposition, but not one which, if circumstances allowed, would create its own *shalom*. Once creation appears, spoliation is the goal; once redemption appears, neutralization is the goal. The Bible describes it in a variety of ways: it is "missing the mark"; it is "pushing beyond the boundary"; it is "injustice" or "unrighteousness"; it is "lawlessness"; it is "faithlessness."

Sin exists in the value system of every culture, so that embedded customs preserve distortions of morality, or welcome an unworthy adoration of individuals, groups, or nation-states, or avoid covenantal agreements with other humans and with God. In every society it becomes built into basic institutions and within some laws, so that these become discriminatory and unjust.

The biblical terms used in the New Testament to describe these cultural and structural aspects of sin are *kosmos*, as used by John, and *aion*, as used frequently by Paul. *Kosmos* is literally an "arrangement," but frequently, in John, bears the implication of "those forces connected through their opposition to God." *Aion*, as used frequently by Paul, has in mind "moral wickedness." *Kosmos* is mostly translated as *the world*, as also is *aion*, though sometimes, for example, in Galatians 1:4, as "age" or "epoch"; thus:

> ... the Lord Jesus Christ, who gave himself for our sins to rescue us from the present evil age ...

One function of the world or worldly influences is to produce disruption or chaos within the church and within believers. However "the world" itself is not unplanned or disorganized in its attacks. Its main instrument appears to be *the lure into conformity* of all human beings. It seems to matter little to what anyone is conformed, so long as it is something other than God. In Paul's words:

> They exchanged the truth about God for a lie, and worshiped and served created things rather than the Creator. (Romans 1:25)

The organizer of "the world" is Satan himself, of whom we shall have more to say in the sections that follow. It was Satan who showed Jesus all the kingdoms of the world and their splendor, and who offered these to him, if he would bow down and worship himself, Satan. And it was he whom Jesus called "the prince of this world"—though only for a time (John 12:31–32)! In to-day's language we might well call him the Secretary-General of "the world," because he organizes and does so on a worldwide systemic scale.

And, of course, sin exists in the individual person, being intimately associated with all of thought, feeling, and action. Within whatever habitat, *it penetrates, disfigures, or destroys relationships*: with God, with groups, with other individuals, and with oneself. In biblical terms, it is called *"the sinful nature"* (especially in Paul's Galatians Letter). But this does not describe or represent either God's original or ultimate creative plan whereby human nature would reflect his own. What has happened now to human beings is that they all have an inclination and a propensity to sin, which comes to be expressed in action, and which was seen by Jesus as a form of slavery. For the Christian believer, this means that there is an ongoing struggle—even a near-paralysis—within personality. The Holy Spirit is contrary to the sinful nature and *vice versa*.

This situation, then, may well be disturbing to us, but was infinitely more so to Jesus. To a group of Jews who were proud to trace their ancestry back to *their father Abraham*, he provocatively explains:

> You belong to *your father, the devil*, and you want to carry out your father's desires. He was a murderer from the beginning, not holding to the truth, for there is no truth in him. When he lies, he speaks his native language, for he is a liar and the father of lies (John 8:44; emphasis added).

B. HOW EMBARRASSING!

In our modern and materialistic world, we find it hard to imagine angelic beings who are not quite like ourselves though apparently they have some things in common with us. We normally cannot see them, though we learn from the Bible that they sometimes appear. As a rule, they seem to be completely devoted to God, and even play a part in looking after us; these are good and godly creatures. Jesus advised his disciples on earth not to look down on his "little ones"—either little in age, i.e., children, or young in the faith—"for I tell you that *their angels in heaven* always see the face of my Father in heaven" (Matthew 18:10–11). But though this is "other-worldly," at least it sounds like good news. (Wasn't it angels who brought good tidings of great joy at Jesus' birth?)

Walking Alongside

It seems embarrassing, however, in our age to envisage a Bad Angel, presumably created originally to be a messenger from God, but whose goal now is to undermine the work of God chiefly by attacking the human beings created by God and inviting, or influencing, them to join in sin within the kingdom of darkness. And, as an indication that society rejects such a creature from serious consideration, it makes fun of Satan through a caricature featuring horns, a pitchfork, a long tail, and an alarming red costume. He is now the stuff of a fairytale villain, and can be relegated to the world of Hansel and Gretel, along with an army of supportive evil spirits. All of which suits Satan fine!

Cornelius Plantinga, quoted earlier, illustrates the fact that even some popular preachers within the Christian tradition are so edgy about sin that they redefine it *in psychological terms*. Hence Robert Schuller, for many years pastor of the Crystal Cathedral, defines sin as anything that robs people of their self-esteem. Sin, according to Schuller, is "psychological self-abuse with all of its consequences . . . Salvation is the move from psychological self-abuse to self-esteem . . . The Cross will sanctify your ego trip . . . just as it did for Jesus."[2] What we would object to here is not the issue of self-esteem, but the attempt to use it as a substitute, a gap-filler, for something which is intellectually uncomfortable but profoundly important.

It is not only preachers, however, who show embarrassment. According to Gilbert Meilaender, some prominent theologians also avert their gaze. Meilaender asserts:

> Schleiermacher did his best to eliminate belief in the Devil. Certainly, he conceded, Jesus referred to the Devil from time to time, but only in an offhand manner, and then only to accommodate himself to the superstitious way people talked in those days. The assumption is that *Jesus must have known better, otherwise he would not meet the standards of our enlightened age.*[3]

In the passage that comes towards the end of the next section (2), the reader is invited to judge whether Jesus was speaking "in an offhand manner," or, alternatively, was accommodating himself to the thought-forms of his hearers in a way adjusted to their superstitious expectations. One of the issues at stake in the passage, and a central one, was *truth*. The question to answer is whether accommodation to superstition can pass for truth.

---

2. Ibid., 102, fn11. Plantinga is quoting from Schuller, *Self-Esteem*.
3. Meilaender, "I Renounce the Devil and All His Ways", 95. Emphases added.

Angels, good or bad, come in and out of favor over the centuries in the popular view, and if out-of-favor, they are likely to be thought an embarrassment; but the same has often been true of scientific discoveries. Fortunately the social acceptability of belief is not one of the criteria of truth!

In the meantime we return to *shalom*, the way things are supposed to be, but especially to look at the Prince of shalom, the Prince of peace.

C. HOW VERY SERIOUS!

Jesus talked, within the gospel stories, about sin, Satan, and demons as though they were real and active. But it is against the backdrop of *who Jesus was* that sin is to be basically discerned. He was a genuine human being, having most things in common with other humans, and was not, as Professor John Anderson of Sydney University thought Christians believed, "half a man and half a God." The theologian, Archdeacon T.C. Hammond, who, in 1942, was debating Anderson, gave the memorable response: "The church has always believed that Jesus was *fully man and fully God!*" To this we may add that Jesus, the God–Man, was *fully good*.

1. Seeing God and seeing self

There is an extraordinary story in the book of Isaiah, where Isaiah himself saw the Lord, and also heavenly creatures known as seraphs. They were calling to one another:

> "Holy, holy, holy is the Lord Almighty;
> the whole earth is full of his glory."
> "Woe to me!" I cried. "I am ruined! For I am a man of unclean lips, and I live among a people of unclean lips, and my eyes have seen the King, the Lord Almighty." (Isaiah 6:3b,5)

A parallel story in the Gospel of Luke concerns Simon Peter, the fisherman plying his trade at the Sea of Galilee. Jesus got into Simon's boat, which was then pulled out a little from the shore, and continued to teach the people who had gathered around him. When he finished teaching, Jesus told Simon to put out into the water and let down the nets. Simon, the expert, said that he and his companions had worked all through the night and had caught nothing, but would comply because Jesus had given the instruction. The result was that so many fish were caught that the nets began to break.

> When Simon Peter saw this, he fell at Jesus' knees and said, "Go away from me, Lord; I am a sinful man!" (Luke 5:3–8)

When Isaiah saw the Lord, the Holy One in his heavenly glory, Isaiah's immediate response was to see himself, in contrast, not as weak, or limited, or incompetent, but as *a sinner*.

When Peter saw Jesus in his human glory, Peter likewise glimpsed something of Jesus' care and holiness; and, in contrast, *his own lack of trust, his sin*. In both cases, it was the revelation of holiness that provoked the recognition of personal sin; and, in Isaiah's case, also of corporate sin. It is also interesting, that following the confession of sin, there was a significant commissioning. In Isaiah's case it was "Go and tell this people." In Peter's case it was "From now on you will fish for people." The Holy One had both acted and spoken!

2. Son, sin, and slavery

On a number of occasions, Jesus was involved in high and public controversy with the devout Jews of his time, who found him anything but orthodox. In John 8:31–47, there is a concentration of teaching about sin and the devil, about Jesus' own character, and the vital role, with respect to sin or truth, of trusting and belonging. It is in this passage also that we can test the cogency of Schleiermacher's view introduced earlier.

> Jesus said, "If you hold to my teaching, you are really my disciples. Then you will know the truth, and *the truth will set you free.*"
> They answered him, "We are Abraham's descendants and have never been slaves of anyone. How can you say that we shall be set free?"
> Jesus replied, "Very truly I tell you, everyone who sins is a slave to sin. Now a slave has no permanent place in the family, but a son belongs to it forever. So *if the Son sets you free, you will be free indeed*. I know you are Abraham's descendants. Yet you are looking for a way to kill me, because you have no room for my word. I am telling you what I have seen in the Father's presence, and you are doing what you have heard from your father."
> "Abraham is our father," they answered.
> "If you were Abraham's children," said Jesus, "then you would do what Abraham did. As it is, you are looking for a way to kill me, a man who has told you the truth that I heard from God. Abraham

> did not do such things. You are doing the works of your own father."
> "We are not illegitimate children," they protested. "The only Father we have is God himself."
> Jesus said to them, "If God were your Father, you would love me, for I came from God and now am here. I have not come on my own; but he sent me. Why is my language not clear to you? Because you are unable to hear what I say. You belong to your father, the devil, and you want to carry out your father's desires."

In summary: sin enslaves; the truth of Jesus' words sets free; when the Son sets people free, they are truly free. Some, however, have "no room" for his words. A "father" is one on whom you model yourself and to whom you belong. If God were your father, you would love Jesus because he came and spoke on God's behalf. Your real father is the devil, a murderer, a liar, and the mentor of liars. You neither hear nor believe, because you don't belong to God.

Finally, however, the astonishing challenge from the passage emerges: *Can any of you prove me guilty of sin?*

The biblical record indicates that Jesus' religious opponents were, by this stage, actively searching for something in his words or behavior about which they could accuse him. Now he invites them to bring their charge! They answer only by name-calling, which includes the jibe that he is demon-possessed. Were, then, his remarks about the demonic "offhand," or condescending, or accommodating? Or did he reveal, in white-hot controversy, his own nature, the devil's nature, and the tendency of human nature?

Serious questions, indeed!

D. SIN AND SATAN PERHAPS... BUT SURELY NOT *DEMONS*?

Graham Twelftree has written a number of books on the subject of exorcism and among these two are highly relevant to our concerns: *Christ Triumphant: Exorcism Then and Now* and *In the Name of Jesus: Exorcism among Early Christians*. In the latter, Twelftree ponders the amazing fact that John's Gospel makes no mention whatsoever of Jesus exorcising demons. Instead, particularly in the passage which we have quoted above, he confronts demonic power in general, and grounds release from this, first *in the truth*, and only a little later, *in the Son* who claims *to be* the truth. In his earlier study Twelftree had concluded that the contemporary church "must be prepared to become involved in exorcism; exorcism has its rightful place as part of the whole ministry given to the Church to push back the frontiers of evil."[4] In his 2007 book, which exhibits thorough and painstaking scholarship, his revision is to "concede that the church may confront the demonic in the form of an exorcism *or* in the form of Truth."[5] The upshot, then, is to focus attention primarily on Jesus, the healer, rather than the particular process involved. Having extended the range of confronting evil, however, Twelftree leaves no doubt about his view of demons. Thus, from *In the Name of Jesus*:

> I remain convinced by the testimony of credible witnesses and reasonable arguments, as well as personal experience, that it is judicious to entertain the idea of the existence of some form of destructive spiritual entities not unreasonably designated "evil spirits."[6]

It is, of course, unfortunate that some Christians look for demons behind every bush, disease, or highway accident. This tendency has, in fact, transformed such people and therapists into *practical animists*, in spite of their Christian profession. It also removes from them much of their own moral and professional responsibility. And it trivializes the biblical view within which God, in his chosen places and times, enrolls his angelic beings to do his will, but is also actively opposed by Satan and *his* angelic followers, who assist in evil rebellion. The latter are frequently called "demons," but also "evil" or "unclean" spirits.

In dealing with these matters, C.S. Lewis left us with a piece of sage advice:

> There are two equal and opposite areas into which our race can fall about the devils. One is to disbelieve in their existence. The other is to believe, and to feel an excessive and unhealthy interest in them. They themselves are equally pleased by both errors and hail a materialist or a magician with the same delight.[7]

Lewis is not the only prominent Christian who has given such a warning, and so the following treatment must be as brief as possible, while not

---

4. Twelftree, *Christ Triumphant*, 191.
5. Twelftree, *In the Name of Jesus*, 293.
6. Ibid., 293.
7. Lewis, *The Screwtape Letters*, 3.

omitting things in the biblical record which are important to understand. The New Testament—particularly the Gospels—reveals interesting data about both the authenticity and the characteristics of demons.

1. Demons or disease?

Throughout the Gospels of Matthew, Mark, and Luke, demon possession is normally *distinguished* from sickness and disease, rather than conflated with them, e.g., Mark 1:32–34b. There are several possible exceptions to this observation. One is the story in Luke 9:38–43 about the father who brought his son to Jesus because of his frequent convulsions. Another is the account in Luke 11:14, where Jesus drove out a demon from a man who had been mute.

It has been argued that, in these cases, the first story was really about epilepsy, and the second about psychologically—or neurologically—induced speech interference respectively; and that there is no need to introduce the extra hypothesis of demonic causation. However, if demon possession is credible on other grounds, it is quite plausible, psychologically, that a hostile presence within the personality could trigger the occurrence of epilepsy in the brain of someone vulnerable to it, and similarly that the speech area of the brain could be inhibited.

2. Demonic duress

In the same Gospels *the differential intensity* of demonic influence is noted. In Luke 8:1b–2, it is recorded that on one occasion when Jesus was travelling,

> The Twelve were with him, and also some women who had been cured of evil spirits and diseases: Mary (called Magdalene) from whom *seven* demons had come out; Joanna ... Susanna; and many others.

Along similar lines there is the story, mentioned in several of the Gospels, of the demon-possessed man (or men, as in Matthew 8:28–34) living among the tombs, in the region of the Gerasenes (Mark 5:9–13).

Jesus asked him, "What is your name?"

> "My name is Legion," he replied, *"for we are many."* And he begged Jesus again and again not to send them out of the area. [Luke 8:31 renders this request: "and they begged him repeatedly not to order them to go into the Abyss."] A large herd of pigs was feeding on the nearby hillside. The demons begged Jesus, "Send us among the pigs; allow us to go into them." He gave them permission, and the evil spirits came out and went into the pigs. The herd, about two thousand in number, rushed down the steep bank into the lake and were drowned.

It would be idle to speculate how many demons were required to activate two thousand pigs into a suicidal plunge, or to insist that the number of demons would have approximated the number of men in a Roman Legion, roughly 6000. The point is that the Gospels sometimes report a person being occupied by one demon, or by seven, while at others they report a person being possessed by demons, in the order of thousands. There is, then, an important differentiation in terms of *the intensity* of demon possession.

3. Sensing the Spirit

In the New Testament, demons have *an immediate recognition* of the presence of Jesus himself and of the Holy Spirit, present in his followers. This angelic intuition is coupled with the ability to utter aloud Jesus' identity as Messiah, and also, as noted in section 2 above, to fear his immediate judgment upon them, and to make requests for mercy.

It is fascinating to find a mention of this in the brief letter written by James (2:14–19). In this segment, James is using the word "faith" *(pistis)* to mean "mental assent" or even "mental conviction," as distinct from the way it is normally understood by Paul, as "trust" in God involving the whole person. James argues that mental conviction by itself, when it does not flow through into action, is incomplete or "dead" where personal justification is in view. To his invisible opponent James then says (v 19):

> You believe [you are mentally convinced] that there is one God. Good! *Even the demons believe that—and shudder.*

In summary, it is unusual, particularly in therapeutic circles, to speak about sin, Satan, and particularly demons. However, if a counselor, being a Christian, takes seriously the biblical approach to these, it would seem inconsistent to banish the notion, so that it plays no part in either understanding or dealing with another human being. The fact that Western society has relegated Satan and demons to the realm of imaginative literature or comic caricature is no reason to ignore the deadly serious characterization of them given by Jesus. Satan was a constant non-companionable presence throughout the whole of Jesus' ministry up to, and including grueling Gethsemane. Jesus did not find the devil funny, nor his army of demons innocuous!

E. COUNSELING IN THE LIGHT AND IN THE DARKNESS

The broad but powerful background to all counseling, whether group or individual, lies in the world perspective of the person(s) being counseled and that of the counselor, and the latter may be expected to impact the former, perhaps slightly, perhaps significantly, but usually subtly. Needless to say, if the counselor's world view is genuinely Christian, it will attest to both the *healthfulness* (treated below in section 1) and the *sinfulness* (treated in section 2) that characterize our history and our current horizons. And arising from this there will hopefully be, within the counselor, an intuitive alertness which discerns the parts played in the client's life, both by the light of Christ shining through individual, family, or culture; and by the darkness of sin, Satan, and his agents.

There are occasions when the person has been clearly sinned against, and bears the scars; and there are times where such a person slips into "victim" mode, and now shares some responsibility for the present distress. There are also times where the person has manifestly sinned, and either acknowledges this with a repentant attitude, or resists this knowledge, or is not conscious of it. And one could go on with many other possible outcomes.

It is altogether possible, however, that some newer therapies and even some resilient older therapies have had woven into them a non-Christian world view which is inextricably integrated with their rationale and procedures. Hence the need, initially, for scholarly, detailed, and fair-minded critiques of major therapies by qualified and perceptive academics, especially Christians. I referred, in chapter 1, to two sets of collaborators who, to my mind, fulfill this need. The first consists of S.L. Jones and R.E. Butman; the second, M.A.Yarhouse, R.E. Butman and B.W. McRae, both of whose books have been published by InterVarsity Press.

Walking Alongside

As forecast earlier, we now come to consider both healthfulness and sinfulness as they exist within Western culture, and inform our counseling practices.

1. Healthfulness

There is a need to grasp the atmosphere, the ethos, and the accent that typify the thought and feeling which are ideologically influential in the culture now. First, we shall turn to a view put by Harold Fallding:

> The world has been sweetened beyond measure by the presence of her King. Present in flesh, Christ comprised the standard that every man [sic] must reciprocate or be broken by. Present in Spirit, he exemplifies the standard in a ramifying network of instances. For where His Word concerning Himself is received He leaps to life again by the fact of an answering heart. Thus, by now, countless lights of the world have been kindled at the Great Light. They had so shone before men that these have seen the good works done and given glory to the Father in Heaven. Giving glory to God in this way constitutes a fainter response to Christ which can be called secondary because it is at one place removed. Yet through it whole societies have been christianized. By a christianized society we do not mean one where all or even most members are necessarily believers. We mean a society in which Christian faith and standards are honoured and respected as the authentic guides for life, since persons who exemplify them commend themselves conspicuously and have their path made smooth. We have the fact of christianized societies as one of the evidences that the power of evil is broken and its days numbered.[8]

Fallding, a sociologist who takes note of the varying societies in history, brings us a hint of *shalom* as spelled out at the beginning of this chapter by Cornelius Plantinga. From the point of view of Christian theology, the kingdom of God in its fullness will appear in the future; but since the coming of Christ, we are encouraged to expect that some light from that great day will beam back into our present. It is this that Fallding is celebrating, without in any way denying the temporary princedom of Satan. Jesus himself—and the prophet Isaiah before him—referred to the situation that:

---

8. Fallding, "Modern Christians in a Christianized Society," 23–24.

> the people living in darkness
> have seen a great light;
> on those living in the land of the shadow of death
> *a light has dawned.*
> From that time on Jesus began to preach, "Repent, for *the kingdom of heaven is near*" (Matthew 4:16-17 emphases added).

2. Sinfulness

Miroslav Volf has been called one of the most celebrated theologians of our day. He does not, however, confine his thought within the limits of the library, but is particularly sensitive to the thought-patterns of our era. Having looked back to examine the convictions of Martin Luther in the sixteenth century, particularly with respect to sin, Volf turns to look, in contrast, at the way we in Western society have come to see God as "a doting grandparent." We shall follow him now, in some detail, to profit from his insights.

(a) God—the great granddad!

> Recall the . . . prevalent way we think about God, God as Santa Claus. We make deals with the negotiator; we expect gifts, lots of them, from Santa. Such a God gives indiscriminately and abundantly, for no other reason than for being God and with no other condition than our very existence. When we do wrong—well, we can't do any wrong in the eyes of such a God . . . Faced with human wrongdoing, *such a God becomes a doting grandparent who, for the most part, sees and hears no evil.*
>
> Most of us love the idea of being God's favorites who can do no wrong. We also live in a culture that pushes us into the arms of such a doting grandparent God. First, *we see ourselves as good.* Unlike Luther, as we peel back the layers of our souls in self-examination, we don't expect to find a self tainted by sin. Instead, many of us are confident that, after we have undertaken the impossible task of removing cultural influences, we will reach *our own true core, which is uncompromisingly good* . . .
>
> Today, *a God who wants all our love strikes many as monomaniacal.* And for the self to love its neighbor as itself, many of us think that

it would need to cease to be itself. Our standards of moral excellence are much lower than Luther's. We think that *as long as we don't harm others we are basically fine*. In contrast, Luther thought that if we don't attend to others as much as to ourselves, we're in trouble.[9]

Within these three paragraphs, Volf captures some of the favorite themes of current popular Western beliefs. But he may as well have been talking also to counselors who are dealing with clients who have, perhaps subconsciously, imbibed these beliefs. Some of the beliefs are about God: whether he is indulgent, or whether, alternatively, his nature is holy; and, likewise his standards for his creatures. Some beliefs are about ourselves: that we are basically good, especially when the doubtful influences of a culture have been removed. Other beliefs are about relationships. A Being who covets all our love must be narcissistic, if not crazy; and the demand to love neighbors as we do ourselves is tantamount to demanding our psychological suicide.

There is no suggestion implied here that a counselor should *pounce upon* a client's world view with the intention of correcting or cleansing it. Manifestly we have to work within it until such time as the person can cope with the demands of wider perspectives. Concurrently, however, *we must work within our own Christian perspectives which we understand, and to which we are committed as believers*. To do both of these things is, admittedly, somewhat difficult; but it is not impossible. There may be times, for example, when we might make the comment: "I understand your point of view, and respect it. But I wonder whether you are able to look at it *this way*?" (After all, does not Cognitive Therapy attempt a desired and realistic change in thinking patterns?) If the client is able to look around a particular corner on one occasion, and around related corners on later occasions, it is possible, even likely, that the dots may become linked into a new pattern.

Would it be likely that such a procedure is imposing a new ideology? It is quite possible that a new ideology, or set of beliefs, has supplanted the former ideology. But if there is any hint of *imposition*, the Christian counselor has ignored Christian attitudes towards fellow human beings, and has thus gone too far. When such a counselor has given an assurance that a client's viewpoint will be respected, hopefully that viewpoint will have been *challenged* in a way that is not beyond the client's ability to resist. However, if the client's viewpoint has been battered or destroyed by the counselor's

---

9. Volf, *Free of Charge*, 136–7. My emphases.

authority or power, this shouts aloud that the client has *not* been respected; and for the counselor to act this way would be unchristian and unethical.

(b) Private experience—public affirmation

We now turn to the second and third points of Volf's perceptive analysis:

> Second, many of us think that *what we do in our own private spheres,* especially what we think, feel, and desire, *is nobody else's business,* not even God's. If we act out what we think or desire—if we speak a word that cuts someone down or if we act out a fantasy that harms someone else—only then is there a reason for legitimate concern.
>
> In contrast, Luther looked inside himself to examine whether he loved God as he should—with all that was in him. He examined not just his deeds but his intentions, feelings, and desires to see whether he loved his neighbor as himself . . .
>
> Third, *we believe that we should be affirmed, no matter what.* Affirmation is, of course, what a self that thinks well of itself expects. Anything else can feel like a misreading of who we are, even an insult. We've also come to believe that, for the most part, we don't need to use condemnation to pluck out the weeds of evil deeds from our gardens. Rather, by receiving abundant affirmation, we feel we can water our noble plants, our fair dealings with others, our generosity toward those around us, and the weeds will take care of themselves. Affirmation, not condemnation, is the cure for misbehavior. A God who condemned our deeds would be a bad God, or at least a psychologically unsophisticated God. *An acceptable God is the one who leaves our wrongdoing alone and takes care of our well-being.* A good God is the one who gives us all we need and affirms us and all our deeds.[10]

The stress here, of course, is upon feeling good within ourselves, and doing so with the applause of all other beings, including God; but feeling no ethical responsibility for our inner lives or motivation. At certain times in Christian history, as attested above by Fallding, societies have held God to be ultimately central to life, meaning, and morality. Volf has pointed out that there has been a big shift in the dominant Western view. We, and the comfort of our personal experience, have become central, we are becoming

---

10. Ibid., 137–8. Emphases added.

better and better in our psychological understanding, and if there is a God, he must fit into this contemporary framework. Whatever else he may be, he is no longer Lord!

F. A STRATEGY FOR THE CHRISTIAN COUNSELOR

In the light of what we know from the Bible, from Christian history, and from personal experience about sin, Satan, and his army of supporters, the big question is how to proceed? Of course knowledge is important, as is the ability of coming alongside the client and sharing to an appropriate extent in the client's life; and there is also the delicate balance to be achieved and maintained between the client's world view, and the counselor's, as discussed earlier.

As we have seen, the powers of evil shrink in the presence of God—Father, Son, and Holy Spirit—and in the light of God's truth; but to affirm this does not imply that evil has become impotent in our current world. I mention here, but will not attempt to elaborate, that in recent decades demon possession has entered the Western world particularly in the wake of witchcraft and satanic ritual abuse. Especially where the diagnosis is Dissociative Identity Disorder, i.e., DID, it is not uncommon for one of the "multiple personalities" or "alters" to be a demon which responds to the presence of the Spirit within the Christian counselor in ways reminiscent of the New Testament. A close colleague of mine, who is a highly experienced counselor and was in no way ambitious to confront demonic activity, was challenged, by the situation of a client, to carry out an exorcism and did so, to her own surprise. Since this first exercise there have been other occasions also, but she sees herself not as some high-powered specialized exorcist, but as a counselor who has been called upon to include this special task in her repertoire from time to time. I would suggest that this is a gift not bestowed on every Christian counselor. It will perhaps be useful to record, however, that Graham Twelftree, mentioned earlier, developed a careful form of words which could be safely but adequately used in an exorcism, bearing in mind the cases of demon possession mentioned in Matthew, Mark, Luke, and Acts, in addition to those observed in our contemporary world. In recording this below, it does not constitute an open invitation for Christian counselors to venture prematurely into this field. One must be assured of God's guidance to do so. I myself, for example, have never been in the position of my colleague, and have never been involved in exorcism.

> By the power and authority of Jesus Christ I bind you, evil spirit, and command you to leave this person without harming him/her or returning, and I hand you over to Jesus Christ.[11]

In the long run, the most powerful factor in dealing with the multiple activities of sin will be the consistency of the counselor's personal walk with God. As will appear in chapter 10, many clients will observe, quite acutely, important facets, not only of the counselor's overall personality, but also of the counselor's distinctive convictions and goals. The tendency in the early twenty-first century is to stand light to status and even to the most ordinary of titles such as Mr or Ms. It seems to be symbolic of the need to penetrate to *who the person is* rather than be content with the external wrappings. Thus to some of my grandchildren I am not "Pa" but just "Bill"! I see no problem with this, but emphasize that, whereas this generation finds particular difficulties in "reading" the gospel, it seems to have a surprising capacity to "read" people. The New Testament, however, was well-prepared for this kind of reaction. Christians thus must live in such a way that others will discern something luminous about them and be drawn to glorifying God; and must be partners in the mighty power of God, so that, while not claiming to be without sin, they can take a stand and struggle against the devil's schemes.

Paul, in Ephesians 6, lists the factors that head in the direction of victory, in the face of the continuous onslaught of the powers of evil against the Christian. The imagery he invokes includes the total armor worn by the Roman soldier for purposes both offensive and defensive. An important exercise is to discern how each of these factors should be employed, as spiritual background and motivation, by the Christian, while caring for non-Christians and fellow-Christians alike. For the battle rages as much in the counseling context as in the world outside. Here, then, is the list:

> *Truth*: supremely in Jesus, but wherever else it is found.
> *Righteousness*: being "right" with God, with "fruit" appearing.
> *Support (or readiness)*: drawn from the gospel, the promise of peace.
> *Faith (or trust)*: providing defense from strategies of attack.
> *Salvation*: personal release and continuous growth.
> *The word of God*: (Son and Scriptures) which attacks and penetrates.
> *Prayer in the Spirit* on all occasions, while remaining alert to present circumstances.

---

11. Twelftree, *In the Name of Jesus*, 187.

Walking Alongside

One of the elements presupposed in the overall strategy of the Christian counselor is the recognition of the reality of sin: *sin in the client, sin in the counselor, and sin in the culture.* For the counselor, the great defense is attack, as indicated in the previous paragraph, and for which the simple metaphor is "fruit-bearing." For the client, problems will be posed, and frequently the distinction will need to be made between sin and sickness; or, as is so often the case, an untangling will be needed between the two, to see the situation in its full reality. For the culture and the society, the counselor, armed with insights from clients whose interaction with stronger powers has been unfortunate, may be motivated at least to offer support, or possibly to share in Christian action and reform, social and political.

The previous chapter was concerned with *people*; with how God planned for them to be and to function in his creation overall. The present discussion has brought to attention the unfortunate reality of *distortion* within people, culture, and societies: a distortion brought about and continued by many surface factors, but ultimately by the absence of an intimate relationship with Christ, his Spirit, and God the Father. Even as we recognize the effects of sin, we must be positive; this is germane to our Christian hope. But we must not walk blind!

The following chapter deals with *how people see themselves,* and more particularly, *with how people feel about themselves.* And obviously this question will be illuminated by the scriptural presuppositions about the way things ought to be in the lives of human beings, and the way things are not supposed to be.

4

Self-Esteem

Over the last forty years we have been invaded, assaulted by a new concept "self-esteem," a close relative of "self-worth," and a first cousin of the slightly less demanding "self-image." One might have suspected that Christian people would have greeted the idea with caution; and no doubt there were some who did. On the whole, however, self-esteem burned its way into our thought-forms with an air of conviction and rightness that swept almost all before it. Popular psychology focused on lack of or poor self-esteem as one of our great modern evils and labeled those who brought it about in others as heinous abusers. Is there any truth in all this?

In a previous generation, "Self" was seen as morally and spiritually dangerous, at the very least. It was perceived to be connected with "selfishness"; on the contrary, "selflessness" was much admired. "Self" was in dire ethical competition with "others" and could well be in opposition to God. Recall Theodore Monod's hymn, "O the bitter shame and sorrow," which portrayed the competitive self struggling with God. It records four stages, each of which is defined by the last line of its four stanzas:

1. *All* of self, and *none* of Thee.
2. *Some* of self, and *some* of Thee.
3. *Less* of self, and *more* of Thee.
4. *None* of self, and *all* of Thee![1]

---

1. Monod, *The Baptist Hymn Book*, no.603.

In this recent high regard for self-esteem, what has happened to the self that needed, as in the hymn, blanket extinguishment? Have we been wise to usher the newcomer into the guest bedroom without a heavier check on credentials? Should we esteem it or eliminate it?

A. EXPLORING THE SELF

Had we lived in a much earlier era, that of Puritan England and America, we may well have stepped away, in our exploration, from an honorific use of "self-esteem" or "self-worth." Stephen Charnock, a Puritan, has asked:

> Whence springs envy, but from a self-love grieved at its own wants in the midst of another's enjoyment? ... What is pride, but a sense of self-worth, a desire to have self of a higher elevation than others? ... *Sin indeed may well be termed a man's self ... Sin and self are all one.*[2]

At face value, then, self-worth for the Puritans not only was *not* the great boon that it has been thought to be in the late twentieth and early twenty-first centuries, but was to be viewed as pride and hence sinful. Add to this the emphasis that sin was to be "mortified" or killed off, and the contrast would appear to be complete and extreme. However, to reach this conclusion and to look no deeper would be to ignore the spiritually sophisticated distinctions that the Puritans made within Christian experience. Hence we must give careful attention to these.

Charnock distinguishes three types of self-love:

1. There is "a natural self-love"[3] that humans share with all living things. It is a non-self-conscious concern for health and wholeness, an affection for our existence. Paul referred to this when he said: "After all, people have never hated their own bodies, but they feed and care for them" (Ephesians 5:29).

It has nothing to do with self-image.

2. There is "a carnal self-love." Charnock says it is

> "when a man loves himself above God ... when our thoughts, affections, designs, centre only in our own ... interest."[4]

---

2. Charnock, *Discourses Upon the Existence and Attributes of God*, 153. Emphasis added.

3. Ibid., 152–53.

4. Ibid., 152.

This is the natural self-love which has become "criminal in excess" under the influence of sin. We come to "expect a blessedness from ourselves," an expectation which must always be frustrated.

3. There is "a gracious self-love" which can be generated by the Holy Spirit. It occurs

> "when we love ourselves for higher ends than the nature of a creature . . . in subserviency to the glory of God."[5]

Charnock recalls the view of Paul that a Christian is said to be created in Christ Jesus to do good works (Ephesians 2:10), and as they come to see this as their true "end" or purpose, they will become well pleased with themselves.

While these distinctions are welcome and interesting, there is a need to start again in a more relational context, to review the situation psychologically and then theologically. In starting again, however, we can accept the notion of carnal self-love as both genuine and threatening, and perhaps the most basic form of idolatry in modern times. And we can also accept the reality of an appropriate self-understanding which is congruent with Pauline insights.

B. LOCATING THE SELF

There is probably a time in infancy when one is entirely non-self-conscious, so that even hands and feet do not "belong," but are just objects among all the other things constituting the "big, buzzing confusion" that is the outside world. But then come Mum (very close at hand) and Dad (a little further away), who insist on relating, caring, enjoying, being exasperated with one, and then regularly naming one. At the very least this must prepare the ground for the realization that one—Jack or Jill—*exists*, and hereabouts! Perhaps a lot of this is like the air we breathe, until some event jolts us into self-consciousness, an awareness that *I* exist, and am of a certain kind. I can recall that at age five, in kindergarten, some adult said something to the effect that I was an "unusual" or "difficult" child. (How very perceptive!) I knew quite clearly that it was *I* being referred to, and I knew just as clearly that that woman was wrong: I was not that kind of child! What is instructive about this example is that I had previously had reflected back to me the views of my mother, father, grandmother, and favorite aunt, and had internalized those as being true. Now this "meddlesome matron" reflected

---

5. Ibid., 152.

Walking Alongside

back to me a contrary view, which of course was untrue! So it was out of a growing matrix of relationships that self-knowledge and self-appraisal were replacing the earlier self-innocence.

Even in the light of all this, it would be wrong to assume that self-knowledge and self-appraisal became my major preoccupation in life. What other people were like, what animals and birds were like, what sums and stories and sciences were like, and what God was like, would all play their part in my expanding exploration of life. And emerging from all these, there would be a making, a modifying, a correcting, and an occasional refashioning of the hypotheses, images, or models involved. An image of self, growing mainly out of personal relationships, but also out of attempts to interact with non-personal things, would become clearer, and hopefully more realistic as time went on. And, to repeat, this image would be both descriptive (what I am like) and evaluative (how valuable or worthwhile I am).

Before leaving this brief developmental sketch (which errs, perhaps, on the side of being somewhat idyllic), we must examine a different and depressing scenario. In this case, the developing self is located in a home where, even if there is some subterranean love, there is no *respect* for the growing child. The child is "put down," seen as a nuisance, told they are hopeless and stupid, and either tyrannized or left to their own devices without appropriate guidance, encouragement, or discipline. In this case a stunted self-image develops, as well as a self-appraisal lacking esteem, which in some cases yields self-hatred. Respect, conferred upon a child is like a coin: one side shows an expectation that in the respected child something of worth or value is likely to emerge. (This is different from, and more subtle than, that admiration which showers praise on what has already emerged.) The other side shows a protective self-restraint which is determined not to interfere with or destroy what is likely to emerge in the one who is respected. When there is no expectation of worth, conveyed by the adult to the child, that child will develop no healthful and natural self-expectation. When there is interference, or destructiveness, or mindless indulgence, the child will lack the freedom to grow and to become. The self is wounded and distorted, and in need of therapy. There is, under these circumstances, significant lack of self-esteem.

Return now to the happier case. Children do not have to be brim-full of self-congratulation or smart self-confidence, but are just freer to explore the world and relate to others without an awful "down-drag" while doing so. If ever they were asked how they felt about themselves, they might say

"OK!" but would not necessarily be much more preoccupied with the issue than that. Once again, reasonably "normal" social circumstances are often as non-intrusive as the physical circumstances such as the sun, the air, or the drink of water.

> Your father . . . causes his sun to rise on the evil and the good, and sends rain on the righteous and the unrighteous. (Matthew 5:45)

Normal self-esteem is one of the outcomes of what Christians call "common grace," a gift from God, conveyed, in this case, through respectful parents.

C. ORIENTATING THE SELF

Both the Old and New Testaments make it clear that human beings, limited and sinful though they are, may join with the angels and the whole of creation in praising and glorifying God; and that God delights in this sacrifice. The Bible is equally clear that human beings themselves are only genuinely fulfilled when they are focused upon or orientated towards God, in contradistinction from any other style of life-centering. The call of the gospel is to turn

> to God from idols to serve the living and true God, and to wait for his Son from heaven, whom he raised from the dead—Jesus, who rescues us from the coming wrath. (1 Thessalonians 1:9b–10)

The psychology of the Bible confirms this notion in its use of certain words associated with persons, as was explained in more detail in chapter 2. As was noted there, in the Old Testament, two of those are particularly pertinent: *ruach* and *leb*. *Ruach* refers to breath, wind, or spirit, which prompts or inclines a person in the direction of God; and *leb* is the heart or mind, or center of being, the nature of which is to be devoted to something or someone—ideally to God. Johannes Pedersen, speaking from within this biblical idiom, expressed the situation thus: "When a man [sic] remembers God, he lets his being be determined by him."[6]

In the New Testament, two words, once again, emphasize the theme of orientation: *nous*, meaning a response to God's message, involving understanding, commitment, and action; and *kardia*, which serves an almost identical function as *nous* by embracing all the same elements, but

---

6. Pedersen, *Israel: Its Life and Culture*, 106.

emphasizing the feeling aspects somewhat more.[7] Both terms have strong reference to the workings of the human ego or self.

But already in this account of orientation we need a corrective. Western culture will usually tend to assume that when we are speaking of focus or orientation we have in mind individual responses. Neither the relevant Old nor New Testament passages would, however, harbor this presupposition. When Isaiah, for example, was confronted with a vision of Yahweh and the seraphs praising him, he recorded this reaction:

> Woe is me! . . . I am ruined! For I am a man of unclean lips, and I live among a people of unclean lips, and my eyes have seen the King, the LORD Almighty. (Isaiah 6:5)

To see Yahweh means, then, that Isaiah perceives not only what he himself is like ethically, but what also his people and nation are like. It is the individual-in-community which needs re-focusing. Similarly in the New Testament, e.g., Ephesians 4:11–13. As dealt with in Section E of this chapter, the goal is maturity and knowledge of the Son of God; but the process is one in which individual and community cannot profitably be disentangled.

In the light of the factors of orientation and an individual-communal emphasis, we may now introduce a framework which facilitates biblically the expression of such self-orientation. This is to be found in the display, by Nicholas Wolterstorff, of the biblical notion of *shalom*, i.e., peace. In his book, *Until Justice and Peace Embrace*, Wolterstorff outlines his analysis as follows:

> Shalom in the first place incorporates right, harmonious relationships to *God* and delight in his service . . . Secondly, shalom incorporates right harmonious relationships to other *human beings* and delight in human community . . . Thirdly, shalom incorporates right, harmonious relationships to *nature* and delight in our physical surroundings . . . Shalom is more than an ethical community. Shalom is the responsible community in which God's laws for the multifaceted existence of his creatures are obeyed . . . In summary, shalom is the human being dwelling at peace in all his or her relationships: with God, with self, with fellows, with nature.[8]

---

7. See Ridderbos, *Paul*, 117–120.
8. Wolterstorff, *Until Justice and Peace Embrace*, 69–71.

Self-Esteem

Wolterstorff's final observation is, however, that "peace" (*shalom*)—this web or complex of relationships in which the criterion of being "right and harmonious" is based squarely in love, faithfulness, and justice—points to Jesus Christ whom Isaiah, in anticipation, called "Prince of Peace" (Isaiah 9:6).

In a developmental and a scriptural sense, then, the "self" is constituted by the presence or absence of personal relationships (the coming into being of the self-in-community), and then is orientated, focused, and ultimately characterized by the presence or absence of such relationships (the lifestyle of the self-in-community). There is considerable profit to be gained, at this point, in tracing the history of how the "self" has been seen over past centuries and on the current scene. Space prevents even a summary here of the detailed changes surrounding the concept. A masterly treatment of this history has been given, however, by Stanley Grenz, in chapter 2 of his book, *The Social God and the Relational Self*. Appropriate to its content, the sub-title of the chapter is *An Archaeology of the Self*.

D. EMPLOYING THE SELF

A highly significant passage for our quest is Romans 6:11–13:

> . . . count yourselves dead [completely unresponsive] to sin, but alive [alertly responsive] to God in Christ Jesus. Therefore do not let sin reign in your mortal body so that you obey its evil desires. Do not offer any part of yourself to sin as an instrument of wickedness, but rather offer yourselves to God as those who have been brought from death to life; and offer every part of yourself to him as an instrument of righteousness.

First note the statement of orientation given in the first sentence of the quotation. If believers are ready, in lively responsiveness to God, to offer themselves and aspects of themselves—knowledge, skills, experience, wisdom, and especially "grace-gifts"—to God for him to employ, then surely they must be able to think about themselves and their attributes, and make some judgments about themselves as instruments which are appropriate in the circumstances. In terms used above, they must be able to develop a self-image which is both descriptive and evaluative.

In the same letter to the Roman Christians, Paul makes this point quite explicitly:

> Do not think of yourself more highly than you ought, but rather think of yourself with sober judgment, in accordance with the faith God has distributed to each of you. (Romans 12:3b)

Clearly the Spirit-person, who has the mind of Christ, and makes judgments about *all* things (1 Corinthians 2:15–16) is meant to include self among the "all things." The Christian living within the community of the Spirit (1 Corinthians 2:6–7) aims to dwell in peace, not only with God, with fellows, and with nature, but also *with self.* Such would appear to be acknowledged by Paul.

In the Romans 12 passage, however, Paul sees the possibility of *self-importance* or spiritual competitiveness emerging within the community; and to allow this to become acceptable within self-appraisal would be to succumb to subtle sinfulness, out of kilter with *shalom,* and destructive of the community's fabric. And it is precisely at this point that we can locate the unease of many Christians about self-image: that evaluation of oneself involves a subtle but central temptation to sin. Paul, of course, had seen flagrant examples of such succumbing in the communities of faith that he had founded, especially among the Corinthians. (See 1 Corinthians 2:10–17; 6:1–8; and 11:17–22).

Note now, however, Paul's even-handedness on the issue of self-evaluation, from his discussion of "one body, many parts" in 1 Corinthians 12:12–29. Haughty Eye and proud Head had been known to say to lowly Hand or dusty Foot: "I don't need you!" But if Foot, being put down and feeling inferior, should say to Hand who is demeaning him or her, "because I am not like you I do not belong to the body," though understandably feeling marginalized, he or she would not be justified in thinking himself or herself to be more lowly. Putting together, then, Romans 12 and 1 Corinthians 12, there is a two-way risk in self-evaluation: that of sinning by self-inflation, but also that of sinning by self-denigration.

In such a slippery but highly important arena, where does one go for guidance? Return to the positive injunction of Paul in Romans 12:3c: ". . . think of yourself with sober judgment, in accordance with the faith God has distributed to each of you."

The "thinking" (*phronein*) involved suggests careful or studied consideration rather than unreflective opinion, and consideration which includes a moral interest—in other words, thought which is both descriptive and evaluative. The "sober judgment" (*sophronein*) is one that emerges from a sound mind attuned to all the relations of life; in other words, judgment which is realistic because it takes into account how things are with God, with fellows, and with nature in the course of describing and evaluating the self.

The point that emerges, then, is that though it is easy, when perceiving self, to lose connection with Christ (Colossians 2:19a), and hence pit oneself against or place oneself beneath a brother or sister in the community, a person must take on the responsibility of self-description and self-evaluation, because these are involved in offering oneself as an instrument to be employed by God for the purposes of his kingdom. "All of Thee" *requires* the presence and sound functioning of *self*, because that is the way Christ has chosen to be involved in and to work through his church. "None of self" may have meant, in Monod's thought, no self-inflation nor any self-denigration. If it means, however, *no existence,* and therefore no description or evaluation of self, then it is manifestly misleading. The progressive emptying and final extinction of self is not a Christian, but a Buddhist doctrine and life-style, which opposes God's purposes in creation.

E. ENCOURAGING THE SELF

What, then, do we understand by "*self-esteem*"?

In the light of the above biblical account, what could reasonably be called "self-esteem" is the respect and regard we may have for ourselves, or for our gifts and talents, as God's creation and his instruments. In the parable of the talents, for example, what stewards had been given was to be seen as valuable, and was to be multiplied so far as possible. In the letters of Paul, grace-gifts, whether newly formed or transformed out of older talents, were to be held as precious and developed, and used for the enrichment of the whole community. In some cases the gifts were *people* (as in Ephesians 4: apostles, prophets, evangelists, and pastor-teachers) who had, at God's prompting, offered themselves as his instruments. In other cases the gifts were *specific functions* (as in 1 Corinthians 12: 27–30: healing, administration, miracle-working, tongues, etc.) which involved aspects or parts of people, once again offered in God's service. But because the people concerned and the functions involved were seen as part-and-parcel of the enrichment and maturing of the whole body, the members of the body would appreciate and esteem them. And it is only appropriate that, without inflated egos or apologetic modesty, the people involved should share and concur with the esteem granted to their gifts, or to themselves as gifts. Self-awareness may at times be a real burden but it is, after all, crucial to the way God made us.

But what of the way our contemporary world understands "self-esteem"? What of the gloss given to the term by popular psychology?

David Seligman, the prominent American academic, whose current work on Positive Psychology will be discussed later in chapter 9, featured as a critic within his own field, indicating that in the American culture of the 1970s and 1980s, "self-esteem" involved the determination that children and young people should *feel good* even in spite of adversity, disappointment, or failure. As early as 1997, Richard Glover, an Australian journalist, conveyed Seligman's concerns in the *Sydney Morning Herald*, in an article, "Doing it tough for self-esteem." The claim was that when children emerge from the comforting cloak of "You're the best!" and "You're really special!" and encounter the hardness and unresponsiveness of contemporary life, they have no skills for coping with the severe contrast involved. They can then develop depression, not unknown in children from the age of eight years! Seligman's solution included the training of children to dispute "catastrophic thinking" within themselves, and to discover ways of dealing with tough circumstances in which they had not been readily affirmed.

If the culture or "cult" of self-esteem does, in fact, center on making youngsters feel good in spite of all evidence to the contrary, then it is deficient in at least two desperately significant ways. First, it is utterly unrealistic: I am required to feel good in precisely the situations where it would be natural to feel bad; or alternatively, I am so protected that the hostile elements are not allowed to impinge. Secondly, it is reductionist, so far as my developing human nature is concerned, since I am not solely a feeling creature, but also one who thinks and acts, relates to God, to others, and to nature, and who, out of all these factors, must develop some kind of world view. What has been driven home to me, in the course of extensive counseling, has been the deprivation of many young children because of the lack of love and respect given them, either by parents or by the absence of parenting. There is no doubt that these issue in a devaluing of themselves and their possible contributions.

How are we, then, to "encourage" the self?

Two approaches are discernible. The first has been called "educational" in that many schools have tried desperately to eliminate the risk of failure, by removing tests and evaluations from school experience; and have multiplied occasions for praise or affirmation regardless of whether the social context makes these plausible. We might call these "immersion" experiences in self-esteem. This tendency became so ideological that Shirley Maclaine, of New Age fame, was reported to have urged upon the US government that it institute a Ministry of Self-Esteem! Given that this has been extreme, it would be possible to imagine and encourage an approach which was "educational" in the sense that a kindly atmosphere was created within a center for teaching and learning where opportunities for realistic affirmation were provided.

The second approach would be called "therapeutic," and of great relevance to counseling, in that damage already inflicted would be dealt with in the hope of repair and restoration. In fact, currently, in most developed countries, therapeutic activities are carried out for those with fractured or absent self-esteem, in both individual and group contexts. The processes often take a long time, but usually achieve a measure of success.

My view is that the family should be the locus for contributing self-esteem, while the school sustains the emphasis. To place the emphasis on the school for *creating* self-esteem is to place upon it an intolerable burden. Schools will always, of course, profit from developing a family-like atmosphere, but they cannot, either through curricular instruction, or the removal of all challenges, substitute for what well-functioning families do naturally. But as our societies have become more fractured, disoriented, and disordered, therapy has become ever more necessary. Currently the demand for such is outstripping the supply.

To put the matter bluntly, the sect-like "self-esteem movement" has elevated the cultivation of self-esteem to the proclamation of a gospel; and this it most certainly is not, in spite of its assimilation by some theologians, as illustrated in section B of the previous chapter. More realistically, those who encounter people as crippled and stunted in their development of self and self-esteem, recognize this as a disease, like many other psychological states; a deprivation, a lack, requiring skilled attention. Self-esteem cannot be artificially manufactured. *It is its loss* that challenges societies and their families whose lived values have evaporated or gone astray. Counselors have the honored but difficult task of healing and integration.

From a Christian perspective, it is important that parents provide a loving and respectful atmosphere for their children, incorporating appropriate disciplines and restraints in balance with appropriate encouragements, recognizing that every so often love may need to be "tough." It is also important that parents discipline themselves so that they neither exasperate nor embitter their children, resulting in their discouragement (Ephesians 6:1–4; Colossians 2:20–21). Further, a concerted effort on the part of families, churches, and, where possible, schools will be needed to reinstate the qualities of endurance and encouragement, viewed Christianly. These presuppose difficulties, obstacles, pain, and evil in the world as part of our present reality. Such "nasties," however, need not do away with hope or joy. Indeed, it is because of the expectation of future joy that endurance and encouragement function as the "practical politics" of the present. Endurance hangs on to the worthy goal and battles on, knowing that God is above, ahead, and within. Encouragement lifts wayfarers when they have stumbled, and says "well done!" whenever there is a genuine effort or achievement to be affirmed. An understanding of the Scriptures contributes directly to the formation of both endurance and encouragement; and within the community of faith, these, in their turn, yield unity and praise (Romans 15:4–6)

F. SUMMARY

Within the ranks of Christians, there have been those who shrink away from any mention of "self" or "self-esteem" because of the possibility— a genuine one—that a concentration upon self may usurp the place that should belong to God. Among the neo-Puritans there has been an anomalous tendency; on the one hand to identify "self-worth" with sinful self-indulgence, but on the other hand to affirm certain acceptable kinds of "self-love," including a "gracious self-love," generated by the Holy Spirit. In this chapter the latter notion is affirmed, but it is displayed within a wider biblical and psychological framework.

Within the world of popular psychology and New Age intuition, there has arisen a self-esteem movement which concentrates on making children and adolescents feel good and which attempts to shield them from failure and self-blame. The influence of this movement has been surprisingly pervasive, and has drawn to itself something of the authority of "political correctness." In some circles it has been presented as a "gospel," and attempts have been made to incorporate it as an essential part of school curricula.

As revealed in counseling situations, many clients will have suffered lack of love and respect from parent-figures, resulting in the inability to perceive themselves as worthy, or to make an acceptable contribution to others or to society. This is a gap, a void, a vacuum in the psyche—a damaged self—and it can take time, therapeutically, to bring about change. Nonetheless informed counseling can and does make a valuable contribution both to the persons involved, and even to distorted family structures.

From within biblical theology, several significant insights bear on the subject:

1. The human being is made for orientation around or focus upon God. Humanly this is a need, and then a fulfillment; or a lack of fulfillment when the self has become orientated elsewhere. Either way, such orientation is both corporate and individual.

2. Orientation upon God fans out, as it were, to include right and harmonious relationships with other human beings, with nature, and with self. *Shalom* (peace) is experienced as the self finds its place within this web of relationships.

3. Self is to be viewed as an instrument used in the service either of Christ or of sin. In order for self to be an effective instrument, self-understanding and self-evaluation are required.

4. Paul in his letters warns against both high-mindedness and self-denigration, instructing his readers instead to develop a realistic judgment about the self which is both descriptive and evaluative.

5. The appropriate locus for building balanced self-esteem is the family within the church as a corporate body, as has been spelled out in the letters of Paul. Endurance and encouragement are crucial qualities both in facing reality and dealing with disappointment.

G. TRANSITION

Previous chapters have introduced a concept of counseling, closely related, though not identical with the notion as it is used in Scripture. We have then turned to grasp what is said about the nature of persons in the Bible, as they will feature both as counselors and counselees. But because people have strayed, in that they have not lived and acted in the way that God intended, we have surveyed the effects of sin on and within human beings, individually and corporately.

While self-esteem is a significant factor in development and practical living, it cannot be allowed to occupy an inordinate place in the horizon of life. Without doubt, encouragement and repair are needed to restore losses inflicted on self-worth in the contemporary world. There are, however, many other factors in the realm of personality which require equally the attention of the counselor. To repeat: I am a creature who thinks, feels, and acts; relates to God, to others, and to nature; and who, from all these factors, necessarily develops some kind of world view.

We now, however, leave our discussion of human beings as such, and concentrate our attention upon the initiatives of God and the ways in which he goes about his task of engaging with people.

5

Providence: Engagement by God

A. SOME CURRENT THINKING

Over recent decades there has been a great deal of discussion in theological circles about the basic question of how God interacts with his creation, both human and non-human. The fault line of this discussion can be seen in the controversy on whether God actually changes his mind, and whether this capacity means that God is basically changeable, especially when his human creatures repent appropriately. The "open" view of *The God Who Risks*[1] makes much of the dialogue between God and Old Testament leaders such as Abraham, where divine compassion is seemingly aroused because of God's personal dialogue with Abraham, and where, as a result, a completely new form of engagement can be commenced. The suggestion that such accounts display some form of anthropomorphism is discounted, and appeal is made to the genuineness of personal relationship between God and the human being concerned, to explain the change of God's engagement in the situation. Here the expansion, within the social sciences, of our grasp of the nature of personal relationships, and the reciprocity that can be found within them in ideal circumstances, is taken as a new paradigm for our understanding of God himself. Aspects of this view can

---

1. Sanders, J.

be affirmed from the rest of Scripture, and are indeed drawn upon by those theologians who have exhibited the nature of the Trinity as a fellowship. But the further elaboration by Sanders and like-minded authors seems to require our acquiescence, first to the proposition that God is confronted with genuine risk and therefore cannot be credited with omnipotence; and second, that the future is, in principle, indeterminate, and therefore cannot be known, even by God, rendering questionable the predictive prophecies in both Old and New Testaments. This stance, though it purports to make some of God's actions more readily explainable, brings great difficulties when confronted by many biblical statements, such as that made by Peter on the day of Pentecost:

> This man was handed over to you by God's deliberate plan and foreknowledge; and you, with the help of wicked men, put him to death by nailing him to the cross. (Acts 2:23)

"Deliberate plan" scarcely fits well with the notion of "risk," while "foreknowledge" surely suggests the assertion of a determined future event, which happens to be utterly basic to the Christian gospel, and thus foundational for Christian theology. It is not my purpose to argue any further my disagreement with the "open" view, but merely to record it as one influential issue with which "Providence" is currently concerned, and to register my conviction that the general thrust of Scripture heads in a different direction.

B. GOD'S ENGAGEMENT WITH HIS FAITHFUL PEOPLE

> As the Father has loved me, so have I loved you. Now remain in my love. . . . My command is this: Love each other as I have loved you. Greater love has no one than this: to lay down one's life for one's friends. You are my friends if you do what I command. I no longer call you servants, because servants do not know their master's business. Instead I have called you friends, for everything that I learned from my Father I have made known to you. (John 15:9, 12–15)

The outlines of God's providence for his people, whether these be Israel in the Old Testament, or his converted community in the New Testament, are clear.

> . . . the Spirit helps us in our weakness. We do not know what we ought to pray for, but the Spirit himself intercedes for us through wordless groans. And he who searches our hearts knows the mind

of the Spirit, because the Spirit intercedes for God's people in accordance with the will of God. And we know that in all things God works for the good of those who love him, who have been called according to his purpose. (Romans 8:26, 27)

These two quotations do not, of course, begin to cover the richness of God's engagement with his covenant people, nor his detailed provision for them as they pursue, however imperfectly, his plans for their lives and witness. Nor do they illustrate the astonishing ways in which rampant evil within the world is turned around, given the process of time, so that God becomes the victor ultimately. However, these themes are dealt with adequately by many authors, and are readily accessible to the interested reader. Here I wish to concentrate, in some detail, on what the Scriptures attest about God's engagement with those who, at any particular time are, as yet, *uncommitted*; a process partly covered traditionally by the phrase "common grace." While the Christian counselor will probably be dealing, to some extent, with Christian believers, it will also be important to be aware of God's approach to those clients who do not as yet believe, but in whose lives God will be moving, providing, challenging, and calling.

C. GOD'S ENGAGEMENT WITH HUMAN BEINGS IN GENERAL

There are two basic statements within the New Testament concerning what God wants for his created human beings. The first is from 1 Timothy 2:3–5:

> This is good, and pleases God our Savior, who wants all people to be saved and to come to a knowledge of the truth. For there is one God and one mediator between God and human beings, Christ Jesus, himself human, who gave himself as a ransom for all people.

The second is from 2 Peter 3:9:

> The Lord is not slow in keeping his promise, as some understand slowness. Instead he is patient with you, not wanting anyone to perish, but everyone to come to repentance.

There is, of course, considerable controversy regarding how these verses cohere with the passages, particularly in the book of Romans, which deal with election and foreknowledge. The prominent examples would be Romans 9:18, and particularly Romans 9:22, the latter referring to "the objects of his wrath—prepared for destruction." However, a reference back to Romans chapter 1 provides the following sequence: first, God making plain to human beings certain important qualities of his nature which could be clearly seen and understood from his creation, and which were sufficient to draw out their worship; secondly, their unwillingness to thank him or glorify him as God, preferring their own "wisdom"; and thirdly, God's decision, in the light of their sinful response, to give them over to its degrading outcomes. So while it is true that human beings are without excuse, it is also true that God took the initiative in revealing crucial aspects about himself; and the latter is certainly compatible with his wanting all people to come to a knowledge of the truth and, indeed, doing so *with great patience*, as the reference from 2 Peter affirms. God's timeless lordship and knowledge are rendered all the more remarkable as we now examine the detail of his interaction with his reluctant creatures.

D. GOD'S PROVISION AND COMMUNICATION

Creation, as mentioned above, is intended to be the eloquent communicator of its maker's character, especially his *eternal power and divine nature*. In Psalm 19, David says that the heavens *declare* God's glory, the skies *proclaim* the work of his hands, they *pour forth speech*, and they *display* knowledge. And this communication is universal, for their voice goes out *into all the earth*, their words *to the ends of the world*. Thus David anticipates Paul.

When David considers the communicative heavens, however, his wonder leads him to a contrast, as in Psalm 8. Humans are tiny when compared with the huge heavens, and David is moved therefore to ask:

> What are mere mortals *that you are mindful of them,* human beings *that you care for them*?

God, then, is both thoughtful about and caring for his human creatures.

This assertion of God's active consideration and care for human beings is in marked contrast with both the ancient Epicureans, who taught that celestial beings lived in eternal calm and did not care about the lives of human beings; and from the modern deists, who believe that God, once having created humans, then left them and the universe severely alone.

In this connection we note also the enigmatic statement in the prologue to John's Gospel:

> In him [the Word] was life, and that life was *the light of all people.*
> The light shines in the darkness, and the darkness has not overcome it. (John 1:4,5)

It would seem impossible to pin down any precise application of the first sentence, but it is inescapable that John intended this as a significant blessing given by God, through his Son, to *the whole of humankind,* and that such blessing would be aptly symbolized by "life" and "light." Then, as possibly the supreme example of the insight given in the second sentence, we add Peter's ironic and tragic declaration: "You killed *the author of life,* but God raised him from the dead" (Acts 3:15a).

It must have seemed, at one point, that the creative communicator had been snuffed out; but God's extraordinary action ensured the reverse.

E. GOD'S SURVEILLANCE AND PENETRATION

From Psalm 33:13–15, we discern not only communication, but active and purposeful surveillance and evaluation on God's part. Thus:

> From heaven the LORD looks down
> and sees all humankind;
> from his dwelling place *he watches*
> *all who live on earth—*
> he who forms the hearts of all
> *who considers everything they do.*

In this poem we have an extraordinary juxtaposition. It affirms, first, the continuing creative activity of God with respect to his human creatures, and also his evaluation of their responsible action. In the process, however, we note that it is not only the physical bodies of humans that God has created, but *the hearts* of all, or what we might now call our identity. Secondly, it points towards humans having an existence which is responsible, like God's, but sufficiently distinctive *to be related* to him rather than being *a part* of him, or *determined,* puppet-like, by him. Thus the quality of a distinctive human existence lies open to the judgment and evaluation of God.

God, then, contributes through interaction; and he sees and evaluates! There is, however, a further stage in God's interaction with human beings: *he penetrates.*

In Psalm 7:6–9, David implores Yahweh as follows:

> Arise, Lord, in your anger;
> rise up against the rage of my enemies.
> Awake, my God; decree justice.
> Let the assembled peoples gather around you,
> while you sit enthroned over them on high.
> Let the Lord judge the peoples.
> Vindicate me, Lord, according to my righteousness,
> according to my integrity, O Most High.
> Bring to an end the violence of the wicked
> and make the righteous secure—
> *you, the righteous God*
> *who probes minds and hearts.*

When David makes a statement that God "probes minds and hearts," this might be thought to refer solely to those, like himself, who were in communion with God; or even to Israel, the people of God, in whatever spiritual state they were. However, the context requires that the declaration is clearly more inclusive, for David's reference to "the peoples" would certainly have included the Gentile nations, even if not, as is more likely, pointing directly to them. Hence God in his righteousness searches or probes the minds and hearts *of all people.*

Out of all this an important question arises in connection with the experience of non-Christian counselees. We have asserted aspects of God's providence through his communication, his surveillance, and his searching penetration of all human beings.

Is it conceivable that this makes no conscious, or semi-conscious, intuitive impact upon the everyday experience of people, especially on people who do not yet profess faith in Christ?

F. GOD REACHING OUT THROUGH HIS SON

The provision of God for non-Jewish, i.e., Gentile people and his communication with them would manifestly be incomplete if it did not include the person and messages of Jesus Christ himself, and the way he related to such people. Hence there follow a number of stories from the Gospels which illustrate his way of reaching out. Before launching into these, however, several points need to be clarified. At least one of the Gentile figures encountered by Jesus may have been a "God-fearer," that is a person who, though not a Jewish proselyte, nevertheless had an admiration for Jewish Scriptures, and possibly some acquaintance with them. Some other

Gentiles, not included in this category, may also have been acquainted with Jewish customs and forms of address. Whatever the gradations, however, none of those to be discussed could have been described as "heirs of the covenant" in the traditional Jewish sense, or educated in the Scriptures, in the normal Jewish way.

1. Care for a Roman soldier

In Matthew's Gospel (8:5–13) we are introduced to a Roman centurion, concerned about his paralyzed and suffering servant. This Gentile officer had obviously, in view of his informed and confident approach, become aware of Jesus as person and healer and hence asked for his help. Jesus now offers to visit the servant and heal him. The centurion, on two occasions, calls Jesus "Lord," which raises the question whether this was a polite form of address—perhaps the equivalent of "Sir"—or perhaps a recognition of something more. The story reveals that the centurion combined, within himself, an appropriate use of authority and a deep compassion for those under his own control. He now restrains Jesus from coming to his house, asking him instead just to pronounce an authoritative healing word. It is his explanation for this preference which is illuminating.

> "I myself am a man under authority, with soldiers under me. I tell this one, 'Go,' and he goes; and that one, 'Come,' and he comes. I say to my servant, 'Do this,' and he does it."

Jesus was astonished at his reply and declared, with great emphasis, that he had not found anyone in Israel with such great faith! In what, then, did the centurion's belief and trust consist? It seems that a man, who was both compassionate and also used to being in authority, recognized one who supremely modeled the ethic that he himself owned and tried to live by. He now placed himself under that authority and expected that compassion. Thus "Lord" clearly signified willing submission and trust, rather than mere politeness. Jesus recognized this and affirmed it by saying: "Go! Let it be done *just as you believed it would.*"

2. Care for the demon-possessed Gentiles

In marked contrast from this story is that of the Gentile pig-raisers in the region of the Gadarenes. (Matthew 8:28–34). Faced by two demon-possessed men, and challenged verbally by the demons themselves to send them into the herd of pigs, Jesus agreed!

> He said to them, "Go!" So they came out and went into the pigs, and the whole herd rushed down the steep bank into the lake and died in the water. Those tending the pigs ran off, went into the town and reported all this, including what had happened to the demon-possessed men.

In considerable consternation the townspeople pleaded with Jesus to leave; which he did. *Their* response to his compassion and authority ended up as *fear*—not faith.

3. Care for a Gentile woman

A further fascinating story (Matthew 15:21–28) was played out in the region of Tyre and Sidon—clearly Gentile territory. This time a Canaanite woman from that area cried out to Jesus telling him that her daughter was suffering terribly from demon-possession. Like the centurion, she called Jesus "Lord," but curiously added the Jewish title "Son of David." Presumably she knew something about the faith of her Jewish neighbors. To what extent, we can only speculate.

Following a period of silence, Jesus now appears to give the woman a rough answer. His first comment: "I was sent only to the lost sheep of Israel" — that is, not to Canaanites!

Then: "It is not right to take the children's bread and toss it to the dogs."

One might well conclude that Jesus was testing her in some way. She responded, however, not only with charming repartee, but with the (justified) anticipation of Jesus' compassion. And she was not disappointed! Jesus not only granted her request, so that her daughter was healed immediately, but also observed that *she had great faith*. In what did this faith consist? In most ways, her faith was like that of the centurion. She had a desperate need; she was at least reasonably informed regarding the Jewish faith; she had heard of Jesus and his healing powers; she had met him; and was now pleading her case strongly.

4. Care for a foreigner

Luke brings us the story of ten lepers (17:11–19). These men cried out to Jesus to have pity on them. This he did by challenging them to show themselves to the priests, who could validate their healing. Such action would necessitate belief, because it was only as they went that they were healed. Presumably nine out of the ten were Jewish whose faith was borne out at least against the background of scriptural understandings. The tenth, however, was a Samaritan, described by Jesus as "a foreigner." When he realized he had been healed, he left his nine companions, came back praising God in a loud voice, threw himself at Jesus' feet, and thanked him. Jesus, having enquired about the response of the other nine, explained to this foreigner that his faith had made him well. In what did the Samaritan's faith consist? Like the other nine, he had recognized the compassion and authority of Jesus. Unlike them, *he displayed his heartfelt gratitude*; and in spite of his limited view of God, recognized God's hand in the action of Jesus, and praised him vociferously on this account. Much of this seems to have been intuitive, incipient, "like a grain of mustard seed," but for Jesus it was *sufficient*!

5. Care for a courtier

John tells us (4:46–53) that on a trip to Cana in Galilee, Jesus met a royal official, presumably in the service of King Herod, whose son was lying sick quite a distance from Cana, at Capernaum, on the shore of the Sea of Galilee. Stories about Jesus' healings during the recent Passover feast had been circulating around Galilee at that time. As the son was near the point of death, the official approached Jesus and said: "Sir, come down before my child dies." Jesus' reply was immediate and conclusive: "Go. Your son will live."

John's account becomes quite explicit at this point:

> The man took Jesus at his word and departed. While he was still on the way, his servants met him with the news that his boy was living. When he inquired as to the time when his son got better, they said to him, "Yesterday, at one in the afternoon, the fever left him." Then the Father realized that this was the exact time at which Jesus had said to him, "Your son will live." So *he and his whole household believed*.

This story is fascinating for several reasons. First, the royal official may only have known of Jesus by hearsay, but his personal need pushed him to seek Jesus out. Second, when Jesus told him to go because his son would live, he went; and once again *faith was revealed through appropriate action.* Third, when the timing of the miracle had been confirmed, his initial faith was broadened and deepened, along with that of all his household.

6. Care for a woman of failed relationships

One of the stories on which John lavishes the greatest number of words and the greatest amount of detail is that of Jesus' encounter with a Samaritan woman (4:4–26; 39–42). With strong providential overtones, this story can be seen as a case of Jesus actively pursuing a personal response from a woman marginalized by her own people, and initially uninterested in what a visiting Jewish teacher might have to say. When Jesus requests from her a drink of water, her response is understandable enough. Because Jews did not associate with Samaritans, the request was odd! However, the strangeness was compounded by the teacher making the drawing of water, and indeed thirst itself, metaphors of something more personal. And for a Jewish man to speak to a woman in this way was even more odd!

The woman insists on interpreting Jesus' words literally, questioning the practicality of what he has offered. Rather than being drawn away from his point, Jesus persists with his metaphor, which he now transforms into a personal invitation:

> . . . those who drink the water I give them will never thirst. Indeed, the water I give them will become in them a spring of water welling up to eternal life.

The woman now appears responsive to the invitation, although still interpreting it literally; or perhaps she is merely being evasive? Jesus becomes even more personal, perhaps intrusive, asking her to call her husband, and thus revealing her sexual complexity and likely impurity. In a last desperate attempt to escape, she resurrects a popular theological difficulty which may well distract the rabbi in front of her: *where should we worship?* Jesus surmounts this issue which is rooted only locally, and proclaims instead: "God is spirit, and his worshipers must worship in the Spirit and in truth."

Providence: Engagement by God

Finally the woman relegates these issues to the unknown future: "I know that Messiah (called Christ) is coming. When he comes, he will explain everything to us."

With compelling simplicity Jesus tells her: "I, the one speaking to you—I am he."

Interestingly, John does not follow this interaction with any direct statement of her commitment. As in some other cases that we have reviewed, however, it is her action that reveals her faith. Because of her words Jesus is urged to stay several days and, through his further words, many of the Samaritans become believers. They affirm that now their belief rests, not solely on what she had told them, but on what they had heard for themselves. In their own words, they had come to trust the Savior, not only of the Jews, but of the world. But the suggestion is very strong that their faith followed on from hers, and that Jesus' final self-revelation had removed the last vestiges of her resistance.

In what did *this* woman's faith consist? Like several of the other instances already discussed, she had a desperate need; but unlike the others was not initially keen to display it to Jesus. In this case, it was he who brought it to the fore, took all the initiative, and declared himself to be the good news. It was she who ultimately responded with such wholehearted fervor that those who knew her and her difficulties well came with expectation and an openness to faith.

Throughout these examples from the Gospels we still have the picture, as in the Old Testament, of God communicating his nature, but this time through his Son-in-the-flesh; exhibiting his compassionate authority, sometimes responding to the initiative of those in need, but sometimes himself taking the initiative in pursuing and providing for the needy. The responses were sometimes vocal and explicit, while at other times they were implicit in trust and action.

The question will arise about the experience of non-Christian counselees *in our generation.* Some of these will have heard of Jesus through their upbringing, or some form of religious instruction, while an increasing number may be entirely unaware of the Gospel accounts. If needs are of a moral kind, where a client in distress yearns for forgiveness, then Christian counselors may well be prompted to convey something of who Jesus was and is, along with the significance of his dying and rising again. And the same may be true where there is deep *angst,* or a vacuum in personal relationships needing to be filled. More on this issue will be discussed carefully in chapter 10. But at this stage, whatever has been said can by no means justify an approach to counseling which looks for little else but opportunities to evangelize. To talk about Jesus must function as a genuine contribution to therapy or to associated goals of counseling. It must never be a cover for proselytization *per se*. The "prompting," mentioned above, will come in the convergence of genuine need on the part of the client, and a request from a client, to be assisted by the personal resources that he or she has observed and admired in you, the counselor. (Obviously this is much more likely in longer-term rather than shorter-term counseling.)

The words of Paul in his first letter to the Christians in Thessalonica are most apposite here:

> . . . our gospel came to you not simply with words but also with power, with the Holy Spirit and deep conviction. *You know how we lived among you for your sake.* You became imitators of us and of the Lord. (1 Thess: 5,6)

The right to enter into Christian conversation with a client must be exercised with the client's consent, with clear relevance to the client's problems and goals, with proper restraint and with a faith that is lived transparently.

G. GOD'S ENGAGEMENT WITH EXTRA-BIBLICAL THINKING

We now make a great leap from a biblical stance to that held by some Greek thinkers in the first century of the Christian era. Paul, the apostle to the Gentiles, having arrived in Athens, enters into strong dialogue particularly with Epicurean and Stoic philosophers. With great skill he discerns what common ground exists between the teachings of the Old Testament and of Jesus Christ, on the one hand, and those of the philosophic schools, whose spokespersons were confronting him, on the other. On this basis he expounds his apologetic, and concludes by preaching Christ and the resurrection. Although his *approach* is remarkable and exemplary, it proves to be *the content* of what he says before the Areopagus that is relevant to our present interest. Dean Flemming, in his book, *Contextualization in the New Testament*, describes Paul's address as follows:

> Carefully preparing the soil, he begins with universal themes with which his audience can identify: God's creation and care for the world, God's nearness to humanity, and people's aspirations to

Providence: Engagement by God

seek and to know God. Instead of directly citing Scripture, he finds points of contact in their philosophy and literary traditions.[2]

When Paul declared that from one man God "made all the nations" and "marked out their appointed times in history and the boundaries of their lands" (Acts 17:26), the reference is not to nation states as we understand them today, but rather to discernibly distinct groups of people. The mention, however, of "appointed times in history and the boundaries of their lands" is strongly suggestive of conditions basic to the emergence of a "culture" or way of life. What now appears extraordinary about Paul's commentary is that God's direct planning of historic societies and cultures had, as a prominent motive, that people "would seek him and perhaps reach out for him and find him" (17:27).

Earlier we noted God's intervention, through a searching penetration of the hearts of human beings, presumably inviting a positive personal response from them. Here, however, the total circumstances, geographical, societal, and cultural, are also poised towards this end. The inclusion of the modifier "perhaps" allows for the reality of a human challenge to, and barrier against, this inclusive plan of God, by both individual and structural sin. God's providence, then, in such an expanded perspective, is seen to be *universal, personal, and social* in its total scope.

Paul now presses home the point he is making in his affirmation of Epimenides' verse: "'For in him we live and move and have our being.'"

The interpretation of this by the Cretan poet would undoubtedly have varied from that of Paul. For Paul, the words enunciated on Mars Hill, would resonate with his later theological statement in the letter to the Colossian church:

> ... in him [Jesus Christ] all things were created: things in heaven and on earth, visible and invisible, whether thrones or powers or rulers or authorities; all things have been created through him and for him. He is before all things, and in him all things hold together. (Col 1:16,17)

On a more personal note, Paul emphasized, "[God] is not far from any one of us" (Acts 17:27b)—as Dionysius, Damaris, and a few other Athenian men and women immediately discovered. The intervention by a gifted apologist-evangelist-philosopher was among the conditions that resulted in these few people becoming followers and believers; but God's

---

2. Flemming, *Contextualization*, 84.

comprehensive and creative planning, as expounded by Paul, was crucial, *figuring as an effective spiritual infrastructure.*

We now return to an earlier question, but this time in a Greek rather than a Palestinian situation. Is it conceivable, when God has organized societies and cultures so that people might seek him and perhaps reach out and find him, that none of this preparation would penetrate individual minds, consciences, and awareness? Especially if the question is reinforced by the statement: *God is not far from any one of us.* Clearly there will not be a universal response to this universal provision; and that will come as no surprise in the light of scriptural expectation. But that it would *never* be a significant factor in the reflection of counselees, particularly when these people are facing distress, and strongly wishing to make sense of their lives, would indeed be surprising!

H. MAJOR CONTEMPORARY THEMES

We noted previously that Dean Flemming's interpretation of Paul's evangelistic strategy at Athens included what he described as "universal themes." These were:

- God's creation and care for the world,
- God's nearness to humanity, and
- people's aspirations to seek and to know God.

Whether these were "universal" in the sense of being consciously discussed within all cultures at that time, we do not know, and Flemming does not discuss the point. What is obvious, however, is that these themes were of genuine importance both to the Greek thinkers of that era, and to Paul, because of his Judeo-Christian faith and theology. The story in Acts 17 now becomes exemplary for our contemporary situation. The emergent and interesting question is whether there are significant points of contact, say, in the Western civilization of the early twenty-first century, which hold the attention of those who are thoughtful, or even agitated, but not as yet Christian, upon which the Christian Scriptures claim to shed considerable light.

It is at this point that writers such as Alister McGrath, when devoting their attention to Christian apologetics, give an affirmative answer to the question posed in the preceding paragraph. Though his works cover a wider area of theology than apologetics, McGrath believes that the chief goal of apologetics is to build bridges to faith, and to achieve this by discerning points of contact between current thought and experience, on the one hand, and Christian theology on the other.[3] Hence apologetics must be theologically informed, and must be addressed to specific audiences, otherwise points of contact will be too vague and possibly counterproductive.

McGrath identifies six points of contact which have been thought by many to be unusually perceptive, both intellectually and experientially. These are as follows:

1. A sense of unsatisfied longing

2. Human rationality

3. The ordering of the world

4. Human morality

5. Existential anxiety and alienation

6. Awareness of finitude and mortality.[4]

While it is tempting to fill these headings with details supplied by McGrath, it is not necessary, for our purposes, to do so. The point is that we have here an example of a contemporary scholar who is making a very plausible attempt to discover points of contact with current reflective and psychological issues, and to speak to these from the resources of Christian theology. Some counselees, in the course of their conversations, will display an interest in human rationality and the ordering of the world. Many, however, will reveal unsatisfied longings, and many also an experience of anxiety and alienation. Many will bring problems involving human morality, and some will be concerned about their own human limits and their eventual death.

At this stage it is important to recall the findings of Hubble and his colleagues, introduced in the first chapter of this book. Their research indicated that there are four factors involved in successful therapy, the first, and most important of these, being "Client/Extra-therapeutic Factors."

> They are what clients bring to the therapy room and what influences their lives outside. As examples of these factors, persistence, faith, a supportive grandmother, membership in a religious community, sense of personal responsibility, a new job, a good day at the tracks, a crisis successfully managed; all may be included.[5]

---

3. See his book, *Bridge-Building*, especially chapters one and two.
4. Ibid.
5. Hubble, et al., *The Heart & Soul of Change*, 9.

Walking Alongside

There is little doubt that McGrath's points of contact would qualify for a place within Hubble's examples, even though, on the surface, McGrath's list is somewhat more philosophical and serious, whereas Hubble's examples have a somewhat more optimistic note. Both fit the category discerned by Hubble.

If these matters are raised and discussed in any counseling session, they will be tackled from the perspective of *some recognized world view*. It is widely agreed, for example, that Albert Ellis's Rational Emotive Therapy is aligned with the tenets of the ancient Stoic philosophers, and Epictetus in particular; and what is admirable about Ellis is that he makes no attempt to hide his philosophic indebtedness. Sigmund Freud adopted a naturalistic and deterministic world view as the backdrop for his theory of pan-sexuality. The Person-Centered Therapy of Carl Rogers emerged from Phenomenology, whose basic principle is that we, as persons, are the outcome of our subjective experience of reality. And so the list continues. No-one in the therapeutic community can claim to be neutral with respect to a dominant world view. And while some counselees will be less clear than others as to what is most influential in *their* thinking, they also will bring to the counseling room the influence of recognizable, and usually prevailing, world views. Obviously this state of affairs produces some ethical problems for counselors in general, not excluding those who are committed Christians; and this situation will receive further attention in chapter 10.

The overall thrust of this treatment of Providence is that God has taken great pains to care for and communicate with his human creatures, and has done so not only on a cosmic scale, but also in a manner intended to reach individuals within their particular social circumstances. And while there are serious barriers to receiving such overtures, it can be expected that some people will be sensitive to their presence, will see them as personal concerns, and bring them to professional counseling.

We commenced this chapter by identifying Providence as the engagement by God of all his human creatures. Further, through an examination of many instances taken from both Old and New Testaments, we have seen such intervention to be a searching penetration of the hearts of human beings, inviting from them a positive personal response. These insights, however, require us to investigate the whole area of relationships, and, in particular, personal relationships. It is to this task, therefore, that we turn in the following chapter.

6

Relationships

A simple starting point for the understanding of "relations" or "relationships" is the recognition that they are central to the meaning of both Old and New Testaments. No wonder, then, that theologians have struggled with these ideas from the early centuries until now.

A. THE ULTIMATE RELATIONSHIPS

The renewed interest in the doctrine of the Trinity during the twentieth century is normally attributed to Karl Barth who, indeed, took the doctrine to be the necessary starting point for his whole theological edifice. Barth's teachings, however, were criticized and then reworked by other prominent theologians such as Moltmann, Pannenberg, Gunton, Boff, and Ratzinger (later Pope Benedict 16th) among others. Hence it would be difficult to expound, in minute detail, an account of the Relational Trinity that would be agreed by all! However *not* to enter such a rich theological vein would entail a great loss of insight.

1. Perichoresis and the nature of God

Lying behind the current discussions, and contributing to them in a quite penetrating way, is the notion of *perichoresis*, which dates back to the patristic period, in the early centuries of the Christian era. Leonardo Boff explains this idea:

> Perichoresis signifies *the eternal interrelating* that exists among the divine Three. Each Person lives *from* the other, *with* the other, *through* the other, and *for* the other Person. From all eternity they are interwoven and interpenetrated, so that we cannot think or speak of one Person, such as the Father, without having to also think and speak of the Son and the Holy Spirit.[1]

Here we have eloquent reference both to "interrelating" and to "person" within the doctrine of the Trinity. Jurgen Moltmann, recognized as an outstanding figure within trinitarian thinking, brings to the surface a definitive balance between these two terms. Accordingly Miroslav Volf, in his moving book, *Exclusion & Embrace*, indicates the following:

> Though Moltmann (1981) underlines that divine persons are not self-enclosed individuals, but are determined in their particular personal identity by other persons, he refuses to reduce persons to relations . . . to preserve both "person" and "relation" we must understand them in a reciprocal relationship: "there are no persons without relations; but there are no relations without persons."[2]
> *Persons are not relations; persons stand in relations that shape their identity.*[3]

We now return to Boff for a further crucial angle drawn from his display of *perichoresis*:

> This interpenetration expresses the love and life that constitutes the divine nature. It is the very nature of love to be self communicating; life naturally expands and seeks to multiply itself. Thus the divine Three from all eternity find themselves *in an infinite explosion of love and life from one to the other.*[4]

---

1. Boff, *Holy Trinity, Perfect Community*, 111. My emphases.
2. Volf, *Exclusion & Embrace*, 172.
3. Ibid., 180. My emphases.
4. Boff, *Holy Trinity, Perfect Community*, 15. My emphases.

2. Trinity and humanity

The "infinite explosion of love and life" recalls vividly for us the prayer of Jesus, the Son, to the Father, as recorded in John 17:20–23; though this time there is an explosion from God to those humans who trust in him.

> My prayer is not for them [the disciples] alone. I pray also for those who will believe in me through their message, that all of them may be one, Father, just as you are in me and I am in you. May they also be in us so that the world may believe that you have sent me. I have given them the glory that you gave me, that they may be one as we are one—I in them and you in me—so that they may be brought to complete unity. Then the world will know that you sent me and have loved them even as you have loved me.

Here we have a bridge from the life of the Trinity, marked by mutual love and interpenetration, to the life of human beings when reflecting, however imperfectly, the love, the mutual interrelating, the unity, and the personal identity inherent in the triune God.

We can see, then, how appropriate is the title of the book written by Stanley Grenz: *The Social God and the Relational Self*. Grenz's stated aim was "to extend the insights of contemporary trinitarian thought to theological anthropology, with the goal of developing a social or communal understanding of the concept of the *imago dei* as a response to the *dissipation of the self of modernity*."[5]

Thus far we have attempted to capture some of the exciting theological views emanating from Scripture which have been painstakingly elaborated, through proposal and criticism, in the period since the end of World War I. These have given insights into the relationships within the Trinity, including the centrality of love, along with implications for human beings.

3. "Self" throughout time

In the last section we noted the stance, within this area of thought and action, envisaged in the work of Stanley Grenz, and particularly his references to the self of modernity and its dissipation. What Grenz attempts, in chapter 2 of his book, is to display a historical sequence in the depicting of the self—or personality—within Western understanding from the time of Augustine in the fourth century to that of Maslow in the mid-twentieth century.

5. Grenz, *The Social God and the Relational Self*, 3. My emphases.

This brings to light what could be called "an evolving cultural self" or time-related idea of personality, with its own built-in norms and notions of health, embraced by successive cultural epochs. While this opens up a huge area of investigation and evaluation, which it would be impossible to pursue here, one thing needs to be said. As in all questions of culture, genuine Christianity needs to function both as a contemporary healing agency, even among diverse or contradictory views; but also as a prophetic critic pointing away from what is merely customary and conformist.

In what follows, we turn to examine personal relationships in two related but distinctive ways. The first might be called philosophical, in that it examines the nature and functioning of personal relationships. The second is empirical, in that it gives voice to a skillfully compiled record of the place of personal relationships in contemporary counseling.

B. THE NATURE AND FUNCTIONING OF PERSONAL RELATIONSHIPS

1. Roles and relationships

There are many kinds of relationships by which people can be linked with each other. Commercial transactions link people who have goods to exchange; political structures order the rights and freedoms of people, so that those in certain categories discover they have things in common. Legal decisions decree the nature and limits of the landlord's dealings with tenants.

In all such linkages, however, the social system determines which characteristics of the persons involved are relevant in creating the connection between them. These relationships spring into being as *a by-product of the formation of social roles,* and normally disappear when those roles are no longer needed. And a role itself consists of that set of expectations that the interested group holds of the social position in question, and hence of whatever person happens to fill that position.

2. Persons relating: an attempted definition

In the case of a *personal* relationship, however, it is not some external system that determines what one person pays attention to in another person. The important thing in this case is that each person is potentially a world of interest, needing not to borrow significance from a wider galaxy, but presenting to any would-be "explorer" a complex being, within which many characteristics, whether or not unique in themselves, are ordered—or disordered!—in a distinctive way. The focus of attention, we may say, is on what each person *is*, rather than on any task(s) they *may undertake*. This distinction is a highly significant one for counseling, but before it is discussed more fully, it is necessary to spell out in more detail the defining characteristics of a personal relationship. To do this I shall quote from my earlier article:

> It is a connection in which there must be some measure of *reciprocation*. While there may be one-sided or unbalanced relationships, if there were no real involvement of one party, that is, no reciprocation, there could be no justification for speaking of a personal *relationship*. If we now press on to ask what it is that must be reciprocated in, say, a human relationship, then the answer is that it is *a mutual interest in, or concern for* the man or woman involved. In having a relationship of this kind, each party will need *to know something* of the other but, equally as important, each will need *to feel something* about the other. When a relationship has been joined and is progressing, then interest and concern for the other takes on the shape of an exploration of the other's nature and resources; and similarly, if there is to be a real reciprocation, a move to explore the other must be balanced by a willingness *to disclose oneself* to the other.[6]

3. Persons and theories

Counseling, in the early years of the twenty-first century, includes many different approaches as it attempts to find answers to the distresses, anxieties, and addictions of individuals within our contemporary societies. One of these that has risen to considerable acceptance is Behavior Therapy, which is the therapeutic child of Behaviorism. B.F. Skinner, one of the chief exemplars of this movement, has stated as follows:

> A person is not an originating agent; he [sic] is a locus, a point at which many genetic and environmental conditions come together in a joint effect.[7]

---

6. Andersen, "God as a Person," 211.
7. Skinner, *About Behaviorism*, 185.

In the light of what was said in the previous chapter on persons, this statement by Skinner contradicts the scriptural emphasis, conveyed, *inter alia*, by the term *nefesh*, on human beings having agency and consequently responsibility. In addition to this, S.L. Jones and R.E. Butman, in their remarkably fair judgment of the position we are reviewing, claim:

> Behavioral views of the person are clearly *atomistic*; persons are best understood by looking at the "atoms" of their behavior patterns and how these atoms are arranged and related. These atoms are not seen as being held together by, or emanating from, any comprehensive core of the person which we might call a self.[8]

Once again, this Behavioral view contradicts the implications of the many person-words in Scripture which clearly refer both to the "core" of a person, and to persons being held together by the object—God or something else—which is the central feature of their life and priorities. What all of this establishes is that the basic philosophy of Behavior Therapy is inconsistent with the biblical view of persons. However, because therapies, Christian or non-Christian, rarely faithfully replicate, in action, the theories that beget them, we do not dispute the outcome that, in a number of circumstances, Behavior Therapy has beneficial effects.

4. Persons relating to parents

Having picked out an extreme view within the psychological spectrum which, in theory, gives no place of importance to personal relationships within counseling, it is worthwhile pausing to acknowledge positively a movement in the opposite direction. Though having evolved from orthodox Freudian psychoanalysis, the movement called Object Relations Theory claims that each of us carries about within us "images" of those people—unfortunately termed "objects"—such as father and mother, and that our relationship with them and their characteristics has a strong causal influence on the development of our personalities. Heading in the same direction are the emphases of Self Psychology, originated by Heinz Kohut and his colleagues. To quote Jones and Butman once again:

> If early relationships are healthy and nurturing, a stable or "true" self will develop that is capable of mature relationships. If the early environment is characterized by deprivation, however, the

---

8. Jones and Butman, *Modern Psychotherapies*, 148.

resulting "false self" remains limited in its relationship capacity (i.e. the individual cannot value both autonomy and community). A more mature identity is one that is open to input from others without the competing fear of being overwhelmed. Whereas the object-relations school focuses on psychological relations between internalized objects, self psychology goes the further step of positing a strong entity of *self* that is not a separate psychic structure, but rather "might be said [to be] the sum of all these [intrapsychic] entities plus an unnamed integrating function." Such a cohesive and higher-order entity is quite a departure from Freud's original thought.[9]

To the above, we should add the importance of Attachment Theory, to which a great deal of studied attention has been given regarding the effects either of a healthy attachment to the parent by the child, or conversely, the lack of such attachment. John Bowlby commenced this approach with his epic study of children displaced from their parents as a result of World War II; and this has led on to careful observations up to and including the first decade of the twenty-first century, and has been reinforced by insights from neuroscience.

It is very tempting at this point to begin to extend further parallels between the above positions in counseling and what we have learned about biblical descriptions of persons and personal relationships. But to do that would divert us from the point of this chapter, which is *to highlight the significance of personal relationships within counseling generally*. What we have done is to draw attention here to one tradition in which relationships, at least theoretically, play no role; and several others in which they play a highly significant role. Added to this, there is considerable evidence to show that, in *any* helpful counseling, the relationship between counselor and counselee is seen to be therapeutic, whether or not this experience has been factored in by the counseling theory being used.

---

9. Ibid., 95.

C. UNDERSTANDING PERSONS: THE VANTAGE POINT OF PERSONAL RELATIONSHIPS

1. Observing from "the outside"

How must one person be "placed" to achieve maximal comprehension of another person: viewpoint, mood, feelings, plans, actions? Perhaps, as would be the case in observing any object, we should be able to see and hear the person involved, or at least have access to reports from those who could see and hear. Or it might be suggested that we should be systematically connected by structured social ties; that is, in sociological terms, that we should be a role-partner in some social structure. Now it is obvious that by observing a person's facial expressions and bodily postures, and by listening to, and following that person's speech, sighs, or laughter, we would gain some insight. For certain purposes, the characteristics and the actions might "hang together" or "make sense." If they did not, however, and we were genuinely puzzled by what we saw and heard, what could we do to reduce our perplexity?

Presumably we could increase the range and frequency of our observations. But if the one in whom we were interested managed systematically to conceal some important reaction, we could go on with our observant activities forever without getting any further. You may now ask: what about giving the person a large battery of psychological tests? Would not this yield understanding? Without a doubt, the results would be helpful. But in principle, they are still individual measures of a person aimed at quantifying particular characteristics. Even if the test suggested that the person concerned was of a particular "type," no two people who are thus "type-cast" are identical, and their differences could well be crucial if we were to understand either.

2. Observing from "the inside"

Earlier in this chapter I gave a quotation which was an attempt to define the necessary characteristics of a personal relationship. In the light of that definition, if I share with another individual a personal relationship, it becomes clear that it is more possible than by any other means we have considered to obtain an "inside view" of the other, and for the other to obtain a similar view of me. To say this, of course, is not a guarantee that every personal relationship will yield a complete "inside view." There may exist, for example, some initial mutual concern, some slight knowledge of the other and some mild feeling about the other, along with a degree of self-disclosure, while all of this is minimal or incipient. Such a situation has been helpfully described as an "embryonic" personal relationship.

This may affirm the possibility of a growing or deepening personal relationship. Or again, a personal relationship may be unbalanced or unequal, in that, between the two involved, one participates less and confides less, but nevertheless participates and confides significantly. Such relationship, by its nature, is neither static nor readily measurable. It does, however, yield *access* whereas other approaches yield *data*.

3. Relevance and limits

Not all counselors need the kind of inner-personal understanding that has just been discussed. Friendly support, specialized information, and sometimes challenging confrontation are required and these can be offered, in some circumstances, without a deeper understanding of the individual concerned. This will be particularly the case where the client's need is of a generalized or even universal kind. Some addictions, some forms of anxiety, and even some forms of depression may fit into this category. From another angle certain forms of personal relationship may rightly be criticized as unacceptable within counseling. A concern for the client can lead a counselor to the point of losing objectivity; and indeed some analysts have claimed—wrongly in my view—that objectivity is incompatible with being in relationship. Once again, if a relationship heads in the direction of sexual intimacy or reaches that point, it is rightly declared to be unethical by the codes of ethics governing the practice of counseling.

Having freely acknowledged these issues and necessary boundaries, it remains true that many instances of counseling require depth of understanding which the development of a personal relationship is well placed to yield, and from which appropriate access is gained. In terms of the above treatment, it will be obvious, from the nature of relationships, that such access is more likely in longer term therapy; though in therapy, as in normal living, some connections are forged quickly, if not instantaneously. Another important issue arising from the current discussion is the place of the counselor in the *reciprocation* which has been claimed as a necessary ingredient for the emergence of personal relationship. This issue of "sharing" on the part of the counselor has been debated in counseling circles since the time of Freud; it is of considerable importance and will shortly be discussed in the light of contemporary evidence and experience.

D. HOW TO CATEGORIZE A RELATIONSHIP

1. Hubble and associates

One might well wonder how it would be possible to devise empirical research into human relationships. It would seem to be just about as difficult as "catching a moonbeam in your hands." And yet a number of intrepid scholars have approached this difficult task with considerable flair and from a number of angles. In addition, Alexandra Bachelor and Adam Horvath have drawn together the findings of this research in an ordered and illuminating manner.[10]

Before embarking on the task of selecting findings from the above research for display here, we must note one admission freely made by Bachelor and Horvath:

> Relatively few studies have examined the client-therapist interactional process itself—that is, the influence or changes in one partner's behavior as a function of the behavior of the other—rather than separate, unilateral therapist or client contributions. Investigation at this level allows for a more fine-grained understanding of the complex reality of the client-therapist interactional field.[11]

2. Robert R. Sears

The point is well taken. Precisely fifty years prior to the publication of the chapter we are considering, Robert R. Sears, then president of the American Psychological Association, produced a paper entitled "A theoretical framework for personality and social behavior." Here is his simple story:

> ... if a child wants to be kissed goodnight, his [sic] mother must lean toward him affectionately and kiss him. He, in turn, must slip his arms around her neck and lift his face to hers receptively. These latter movements are the ones that fractionate and become

---

10. Bachelor and Horvath, "The Therapeutic Relationship," 133–178.
11. Bachelor and Horvath, "The Therapeutic Relationship," 153.

anticipatory in his behavior sequence . . . these anticipatory reactions to her behavior are the expectancies that make the behavior of the two people truly interdependent.[12]

Within this story, the element of appropriate action is supplied for the child only by the mother; and for the mother, only by the child. Thus the child functions *within the mother's motivational sequence*, and the mother *within the child's*. To accommodate this situation, Sears suggested the notion *of one composite system set up through the interaction of two people*. The term he devised for that was a *diad*, which happens to be one entirely suited to the situation of one-to-one counseling.

Without a doubt the studies that we are about to sample are far more complex than Sears' story, but the crucial factor of interdependence appears frequently, and the emergence of a composite system of interaction, taking shape through a series of meetings, is entirely plausible. Whether or not we call such a system a "diad" matters little. What is significant is that we see it as *an entity*. For this opens the possibility of seeing a counseling relationship not only as a useful context for, or product of, personal interaction but if supported by evidence a significant *causal* factor. This manner of thinking already exists in attachment studies, mentioned above, where earlier experiences of rich or impoverished attachments have been shown to affect the quality of future relationships or behavior.

3. Relationality: non-human and human

This discussion reflects a far wider issue in scholarship generally which has been termed "the philosophical turn to relationality." (See particularly F. LeRon Shults, *Reforming Theological Anthropology*.) Relationality, which is at odds with atomism as a way of viewing the world, is by no means restricted to theology and philosophy, but has also affected areas of science and in particular quantum theory. The following observation from Shults not only illustrates how relationships work, but also highlights the causal circularity in a relational theory. While such circularity would have been a scientific embarrassment in the past, it can now be viewed positively in coming to terms with scientific, social, and spiritual reality.

> Discoveries and developments in quantum theory led to a further outworking of relational thinking; *particle physics is not really*

---

12. Sears, 479–80.

> about particles anymore but about relationships—*interpenetrating and mutually binding energy fields*. After the emergence of chaos theory in the late twentieth century, most physicists agree that *units and relations are distinct but interdependent*: "for an interaction to be real, the 'nature' of the related things must derive from these relations, while at the same time the relations must derive from the 'nature' of the things."[13]

The elements of the above quotation which have been italicized might give the impression that the vocabulary, here used for science, could readily be transferred to discussions of counseling. To accept that would be a serious mistake in that it would take for granted the theoretical identity of physical particles with individual human beings, and of mutually binding energy fields with personal relationships. The very fact that physics and psychology are distinctive disciplines, and manifestly deal with very different phenomena, would render such theoretical identification too simplistic. However, to explore analogies between the disciplines, informed by the tendencies within relationality in general, would seem to be well worth the effort and, indeed, appears already to be on the counseling agenda.

E. REPORTING ON RESEARCH: A SELECTION OF FINDINGS FROM BACHELOR AND HORVATH, WITH SOME REFLECTIONS ON THOSE FINDINGS

1. The commencing generalization, made on the basis of well over 100 studies follows:

> Clinicians and researchers alike have acknowledged the central role of the therapist-client relationship in the process of psychotherapy and client change . . . The quality of the therapeutic relationship has been shown to be a significant determinant of beneficial outcome across diverse therapy approaches, and it is seen by many to represent a common factor accounting for therapeutic success.[14]

---

13. Shults, *Reforming Theological Anthropology*, 18; see footnote 10. My emphases.

14. Bachelor and Horvath, "Therapeutic Relationship," 133. Bachelor and Horvath cite many studies in their findings and the references have been omitted here for ease of reading. Please refer to the original chapter to explore further the studies they draw on and quote from.

In even clearer tones, one experienced researcher declared that developing and maintaining "the alliance" (an ambiguous term referring here to the relationship as a whole, but sometimes only to the early stage of it) is, in itself, therapeutic (and) curative.

2. Characteristic features and outcome effects

(a) With respect to the *quality* of the counseling relationship, the authors maintain:

> Insofar as the alliance [the overall relationship] is concerned, there are data to suggest that its intrinsic quality is an active factor, contributing to the success of therapy over and above concurrent therapeutic gains.[15]

(b) With respect to the *evaluation* of the relationship by the participants this opinion is given:

> Perhaps therapists draw primarily on their theoretical perspective in making judgments, whereas clients may evaluate the relationship *in comparison to other close personal relationships*.[16]

(c) With respect to *participants' characteristics*, the following tendencies are noted:

> Therapists tend to emphasize the role of the clients' contribution . . . in client change . . . whereas clients tend to value therapist characteristics, such as therapist-provided help and *demonstrated warmth, caring, and emotional involvement*.[17]

The mention of therapist characteristics brings to mind the attitudes proposed by Carl Rogers: accurate empathy, non-possessive warmth, and genuineness, which, Rogers claimed, were the necessary and sufficient conditions for a positive therapeutic outcome. Much research has been devoted to this assertion and, though the claim of sufficiency has been disputed, other aspects of Rogers' proposal have been affirmed, at least to some extent. Bachelor and Horvath record their findings as follows:

---

15. Bachelor and Horvath, 139.
16. Ibid., 139. My emphases.
17. Ibid., 140. My emphases.

> Most investigators agree that these facilitative qualities (in particular, *empathy and warmth*) play an important, if not sufficient, role in therapeutic change in most psychotherapies . . . These facilitative variables are among the ones often considered as "common" treatment factors, inherent to most psychotherapy relationships.[18]

3. Empathy

The following observations are relevant:

> Of several therapist variables, including emotional adjustment, relational attitudes, and values, *empathy was most predictive* of being an effective or ineffective therapist. *Empathy also proved to be robustly associated with clinical improvement in patients who were treated for depression with cognitive-behavioral therapy* . . . Related constructs, such as *"understanding and involvement,"* or *"warmth and friendliness,"* studied in the context of the alliance [relationship] have similarly been linked to positive therapy outcome or client satisfaction.[19]

4. The therapist's self-disclosure

Bachelor and Horvath, from the research surveyed, conclude as follows:

> The importance of the therapist's self-disclosure in successful process and outcome is difficult to determine . . . Therapist self-disclosure likely contributes to the quality of the relationship for some clients, but may be less productive with others.[20]

The spotlight comes now, however, on some clients who *are responsive in this area*:

> In clients preferring a sharing type of empathy, therapists were perceived as empathic when they readily disclosed personal opinions or experiences bearing on the client's ongoing communication, with spontaneity and naturalness. The therapist-client relationship was seen as a reciprocal exchange or dialogue, or even friendship, between the therapy partners (e.g., "I specified that it wasn't easy

---

18. Ibid., 142. My emphases.
19. Ibid., 142. My emphases.
20. Ibid., 143.

to live with one's parents . . . He then indicated that at the same age as myself . . . he too had to settle things with his parents . . . I wasn't the only one in this situation. There is a step that has been crossed . . . that of two strangers . . . to the stage of two old friends who meet . . . to 'exchange' about the past week.").[21]

This mini-story would provoke a sense of shock for those in the counseling profession who would consider the role of the counselor necessarily to exclude *a relationship of friendship* with its built-in "spontaneity and naturalness." And yet the story is not merely idiosyncratic, as most practical counselors would acknowledge. Indeed, at the research level, Bachelor and Horvath referred to the frequently cited model by Gelso and Carter[22] in which these investigators proposed that, in addition to the working alliance—i.e., the exchanges of a specifically therapeutic kind—there should be, along with certain other psychological elements, a "real relationship." There has been, of course, some disagreement with the very notion of a "real relationship" by others in the research field, but the Gelso and Carter model is clearly making the same point as that in the mini- story presented above. Bachelor and Horvath make the following highly significant point:

> To us, the development of the therapeutic relationship remains a fascinating area of inquiry because *it merges the human and the scientific aspects of the profession.*[23]

By drawing attention to the above perspectives and findings, we are not suggesting—and indeed the evidence would run counter to such a view—that every counseling interchange does, or should, incorporate a personal relationship which is analogous to those experienced in everyday life. The point being made is that there are occasions in the lives of certain people when such a relationship involving an element of self-disclosure will not only be rewarding and formative for them but may well, in addition, have therapeutic outcomes.

---

21. Ibid., 145.

22. Gelso and Carter, "The Relationship in Counseling and Psychotherapy"; Gelso and Carter, "Components of the Psychotherapy Relationship".

23. Bachelor and Horvath, "Therapeutic Relationship," 163. My emphases.

5. Failure and excellence

The authors record studies in which personal weaknesses in the therapist have been exposed, badly affecting attitudes towards and treatment of clients. In one study, for example, clients of one therapist were liked less, empathized with less, and held to be more perturbed, when they differed from the therapist in their political convictions. Other therapists characterized by high nurturant and affiliative needs, by anxiety or strong affect, tended to display misperceptions of their clients.

On the more positive side, a remarkably clear judgment is made:

> Excellent therapists, compared with therapists in general and regardless of therapy orientation, possess to a greater extent several attributes held to prevent, or at least moderate, negative reactions [in their clients]; these include self-integration, anxiety management, conceptualizing skills, empathy, and self-insight. Two of these attributes, *self-integration and self-insight*, appeared to be particularly important in managing countertherapeutic behaviors, suggesting *that the personality organization of the therapist may be more relevant than therapist skills or focus on others.*[24]

6. Links between present and past relationships

Though many important findings are recorded only one will be featured but that one seems to hold considerable therapeutic significance:

> There is . . . increased interest in how the therapist can function efficaciously as a significant attachment figure for the client. Through a strong alliance [therapeutic relationship], for example, facilitated by the therapist's availability and responsiveness, *the therapist can provide a "secure base" from which the client can safely explore past and current attachment patterns and experiment with new ways of functioning* that can be tried out in the "real world." Indeed, as argued by some clinical writers, the therapeutic relationship may play an important role as a corrective experience for the client. Not only can the therapist help clients to understand their limitative relational patterns better, *but clients can directly experience, in the therapy relationship, a different mode of relating* (including safely trying out new behaviors, such as expressing vulnerability) *and*

---

24. Ibid., 152.

being related to. Clients' dysfunctional interpersonal patterns are thus challenged and can be revised.[25]

7. The authors' concluding insights and overall judgments

> It seems beyond doubt that a positive therapeutic relationship is a necessary (but probably not sufficient) component of all forms of effective psychotherapy.[26]
> The therapy relationship itself can represent a therapeutic intervention.[27]

The editors of *The Heart & Soul of Change* posed three questions to Bachelor and Horvath, the last of which throws into clear relief one of the most significant battles of our time concerning the nature of counseling. Because of its nuances, it is now quoted in full:

> *Question 3. How do you account for the benign neglect of the contribution of the alliance [therapeutic relationship] to change in the formation of psychotherapeutic models? Or said another way, what would you think accounts for the field's obsession with technique as evidenced by the recent attention to empirically validated treatments?*
> Answer: To some extent, theorizing about therapy has come full-circle: From an emphasis on the interpersonal realm, we moved to create a "mind-less" psychology and tried to reduce human experience to small, finite categories and a few universal "laws" about behavior. Most of our current empirical findings indicate a need to return to the more meaningful understanding of our essential intersubjectivity, of the fundamental importance of relationships and, significantly, of the healing potential of a well-managed therapeutic alliance. In opposition to these findings, there is an effort to reintroduce a reductionist mechanical model of the mind (and therapy) in the name of accountability and efficacy. This move appears to us to stem more from political and perhaps economic motives rather than scientific evidence. In fact, throughout this chapter, as we reviewed a broad cross-section of research evidence, we found little to support such a mechanistic view. Most reports we read pointed strongly to the importance of

---

25. Ibid., 157–8.
26. Ibid., 161.
27. Ibid., 162.

the embodied experience of the client ... Although we are both committed to rigorous empirical inquiry as a valuable road to effective treatments, we are equally vocal in rejecting notions that would prescribe narrowly manualized interventions at the expense of ignoring the unique dynamic between the therapist and client.[28]

F. ACCESS TO THE INNER-PERSONAL LIFE OF THE CLIENT

The preceding segment concentrated on research partly carried out by and largely reported from authors who are very conversant with the place of personal relationships in practical counseling. Though their accounts are cautious, there is little doubt that the therapeutic relationship between counselor and counselee is of great importance. Caution has also been exercised when drawing the conclusion that a personal relationship provides "a point of entry" to the self or personality of another.

In recent years, however, there have been extraordinary advances in the scientific and technological possibilities of understanding *the brain* as it influences and is influenced by interaction with the environment and in particular the social environment. The field of inquiry bears the general name of *neuroscience*, while one important aspect within this is called *neuroplasticity*. We introduce now some pioneers in this field, along with possible effects of its findings on the understanding of human relationships.

1. Baroness Greenfield and Pharmacology

Susan Greenfield, Professor of Pharmacology at Oxford University and a distinguished neuroscientist, produced a book in 2003 entitled *Tomorrow's People: How 21st-Century Technology Is Changing the Way We Think and Feel* in which she takes what is called on the front cover "an imaginary leap into what the future might be." She deals with many fascinating scenarios but one of her major themes is that privacy, even in the realm of thought and emotion, may well have dwindled to the vanishing point in decades to come, due to the technological wonders of brain scanning, robotics, virtual reality, and similar procedures. Access to the personal life of the client,

---

28. Ibid., 164–5.

tentatively proposed earlier in this chapter, may then become a *technological* possibility.

Greenfield's book is, in a sense, a warning of a psychological and ethical kind, intended to help serious readers to confront difficulties before being swamped by them. The "leap into the future" assumes an accurate description and indeed transformation of a person's brain by social and cultural means that could conceivably render earlier and gentler influences, such as counseling, out-of-date. And of course it is at this point that a Christian understanding and a corresponding Christian ethic applying to persons and their relationships will be sorely needed by counselors, but also by many others in the helping professions who are concerned with the balanced growth of human beings.

2. Doidge and Psychiatry

Norman Doidge, a researcher at both Columbia University in New York, and in the Department of Psychiatry at the University of Toronto, produced a book in 2007 entitled *The Brain that Changes Itself: Stories of Personal Triumph from the Frontiers of Brain Science*. Doidge points out that whereas scientists of even twenty years before had been convinced that the brain was fixed or "hardwired," and was therefore beyond repair if suffering damage, the evidence had now become clear that the brain has a plastic character and can be molded in a variety of ways by environmental influences, whether purposeful or accidental. The "stories of personal triumph" referred to in the subtitle include those of patients and also those of the highly imaginative neuroscientists who devised ingenious forms of brain modifications to assist them. While some of the therapy was predominantly physical, dealing with such matters as balance perception, memory, and strokes, other aspects dealt with educational retardation, sexual attraction, obsessions, and imagination.

Remembering that the topic we are immediately concerned with is access to the inner-personal life of the client, the following extract from Doidge's book will illustrate the relevance of neuroplasticity to our concern with understanding personal relationships. Quoting Walter J. Freeman, Professor of Neuroscience at Berkeley University, Doidge observes:

> Freeman's theory helps to explain how love and plasticity affect each other. Plasticity allows us to develop brains so unique—in response to our individual life experiences—that it is often hard

to see the world as others do, to want what they want, or to cooperate. But the successful reproduction of our species requires cooperation. What nature provides, inner neuromodulators like oxytocin, is the ability for two brains in love to go through a period of heightened plasticity, allowing them to *mold to each other* and shape each other's intentions and perceptions. *The brain for Freeman is fundamentally an organ of socialization*, and so there must be a mechanism that, from time to time, undoes our tendency to become overly individualized, overly self-involved, and too self-centered.[29]

3. Siegel: Psychiatry, Education, and Mental Health

The point made so dramatically by Freeman is traced through consistently by Daniel J. Siegel, first in such books as *The Developing Mind*, and then exquisitely in the collaborative work with Mary Hartzell, an educationist, entitled *Parenting from the Inside Out: How a Deeper Self-Understanding Can Help You Raise Children Who Thrive*. While Siegel and Hartzell deal directly with the area announced in their title, thus linking the significance of attachment studies to the nurture of children, they also present evidence of brain functioning which has more general applications. Consider the following conclusions from neuroscience:

> With the emergence of technological advances, we can now peer into the functioning of the living brain. As the mysteries of this extremely complex organ have begun to unfold, we are now realizing *how profoundly relational* our brains are. Our brains are constructed to be directly influenced by their interactions with other brains. This is . . . a plastic—changed by experience—and *highly social organ* that enables us to be influenced by and influence our companions.[30]

Returning to the question of interpersonal access, Siegel and Hartzell pronounce decisively on this issue from the vantage point of neuroscience:

> Resonance occurs when we align our states, our primary emotions, through the sharing of nonverbal signals. Even when we are physically separated from the other person, we can continue to feel the reverberations of that resonant connection. This sensory

---

29. Doidge, *The Brain that Changes Itself*, 120–1. My emphases.
30. Siegel and Hartzell, *Parenting from the Inside Out*, 95.

experience of another person becomes a part of our memory of the other such that *the other person becomes a part of us*. When relationships include resonance, there can be a tremendously invigorating sense of joining. This joining is not just in the moment: we continue to feel the connection to the other through the resonance of the relationship. Such resonance is experienced as memories, thoughts, sensations, and images of the other and our relationship with him or her. This ongoing sense of connection can be thought of as *the ways our minds have become linked*. This linkage reveals an integration of two minds.[31]

It is surely remarkable that the hypothesis given by Robert Sears, fifty years before the neuroscientific findings of the writers just surveyed, should have involved the idea of "one composite system set up through the interaction of two people"—a "diad"—and that a comparable link could now confidently be described as "an integration of two minds."

G. CONCLUSIONS

1. A relational theology

Having become aware of the above clinical and neuroscientific developments, we may return now to section A, which dealt with the impact of recent theology on the understanding of relationships, and recall the prayer of Jesus in John 17:21, 23a, for those who would in future believe in him through the message of the disciples. He prays

> that all of them may be one, Father, just as you are in me and I am in you. May they also be in us . . . I in them and you in me.

We may also recall the conclusion of Moltmann:

> Persons are not relations; persons stand in relations that shape their identity.[32]

---

31. Ibid., 64–5.
32. quoted in Volf, *Exclusion & Embrace*, 180.

2. A relational therapy

We have noted a rationale concerning the access that it is possible for a counselor to gain into the personality of the counselee. In a sense, this is nothing new and, if anything, it underlines the responsibility that the counselor carries. We also noted the judgment, by Bachelor and Horvath, that such access cannot be tied to "narrowly manualized interventions at the expense of ignoring the unique dynamic between the therapist and client."[33]

Furthermore there is the emphasis that *spontaneity and naturalness* in the therapist are preferred by many clients, and that *self-integration and self-insight* figure among the characteristics of excellent therapists. Finally there is the suggestion from Hayes and colleagues that "the personality organization of the therapist may be more relevant than therapy skills or focus on others."[34] All of this indicates that it is predominantly what the counselor *is* that is crucial in affecting first, the quality of the therapeutic relationship, and via that, what the client *may become*.

There appears, then, to be a quite remarkable consonance between some aspects of Christian theology, on one hand, and some aspects of research into the nature of personal relationships and brain functioning on the other. What has been hinted at, but not yet explored, is the importance of the attitude brought into a relationship by the person initiating it, and the ethical overtones of such. In both Old and New Testaments, *the centrality of love* in all relationships is of great significance. It is to an expansion of this that we now turn.

---

33. Bachelor and Horvath, 165.
34. cited in Bachelor and Horvath, 152.

7

Love

> What is love? 'tis not hereafter;
> Present mirth hath present laughter;
> What's to come is still unsure:
> In delay there lies no plenty;
> Then come kiss me, sweet-and-twenty,
> Youth's a stuff will not endure.

Thus, in one of Will Shakespeare's songs, a young man asks a very profound question, but answers it with unmistakable affection, warning his sweetheart not to postpone her response!

A. WHAT IS LOVE?

This has always been, and remains, a tremendously difficult question to answer. While many have asked this question for various reasons, our concern is to discover a biblical account of love, and then to discern how a Christian engaged in counseling may express love in the context of the counseling relationship.

Walking Alongside

1. Romantic love

Staying with Shakespeare for the moment, however, we may wonder whether romantic love finds any place of importance in the scriptural record and any affirmation within it. If we turn from Shakespeare's Song to Solomon's Song, the answer has to be "yes"! This time *the Beloved's* response is eager and uninhibited:

> Let him kiss me with the kisses of his mouth—
> for your love is more delightful than wine.
> Pleasing is the fragrance of your perfumes;
> your name is like perfume poured out.
> No wonder the young women love you!
> Take me away with you—let us hurry!
> (Song of Songs 1:2–4a)

2. Sexual love

Theologians in the twentieth century have, at times, pondered the place of human sexuality in God's purposes which aim both to bless his creatures and help them to reproduce, in their embodied life, his own quality. For example, Dietrich Bonhoeffer maintains:

> This belonging to one another is undoubtedly seen here in connexion with man's [sic] sexuality. Very clearly sexuality is the expression of the two-sidedness of being both an individual and being one with the other person. Sexuality is nothing but the ultimate realization of our belonging to one another.[1]

Another angle on this issue is given by Stanley Grenz:

> At the heart of human sexuality is embodiment, which includes the sexed body that marks a person as male or female and out of which other aspects of human existence emerge. Bound up with embodiment is the sense of incompleteness, coupled with the drive for completeness, that together lead to bonding . . . Even though genital sexual expression [will be] left behind, the dynamic of bonding . . . is at work in constituting humans as the community of the new humanity within the new creation in relationship with the triune God.[2]

---

1. Bonhoeffer, *Creation and Fall/Temptation*, 62.
2. Grenz, *The Social God and the Relational Self*, 301.

Sexual love, then, can be seen to be connected significantly with *belonging* and *bonding*, both strong biblical themes. However, having pondered the biblical meaning of sexual love, we now turn to seek the origin of all forms of love.

3. Divine love

An expert Pharisee who wanted to test Jesus' theology asked him: "Teacher, which is the greatest commandment in the Law?" Jesus replied:

> "Love the Lord your God with all your heart and with all your soul and with all your mind." This is the first and greatest commandment. And the second is like it: "Love your neighbor as yourself." (Matthew 22:37–38)

Here the Lord is couching his answer in statements from two books of the Old Testament, the Scriptures of his time. And in response to a further question which demanded the limits to "neighbor," he extended the then conventional range of love. Frighteningly, on another occasion, he further extended love to "enemies," and this not only generally, but with concern for those who carried out his own execution. Such an expansion must also include the "neighbor" we dislike, or is repulsive to us: loving the unlovely!

Following Jesus' death and resurrection, Paul, the great missionary and pastor, attaches his love-references to Christ and the Holy Spirit, and these are many, deeply felt, and comprehensive. Thus:

> I ask him that with both feet planted firmly on love, you'll be able to take in with all Christians *the extravagant dimensions* of Christ's love. Reach out and experience the breadth! Test its length! Plumb the depths! Rise to the heights! Live full lives, full in the fullness of God.[3]

B. WORD STUDIES

A number of scholars in the twentieth century have tried to depict some apparently different kinds or facets of love by analyzing several Greek words used in the New Testament and in other documents of the ancient world; and this approach has yielded some valuable insights. The words attracting

---

3. Peterson, *The Message*, Ephesians 3:17b–19. My emphases.

most attention have been the verbs *phileo* and *agapao*. In C. S. Lewis' famous book, *The Four Loves*, he includes along with these, two other words: *storge*, love within the members of a family, and *eros*, longing or desire, often of a sexual kind. Even though neither of these appears in the New Testament text, the experiences lying behind them can be clearly discerned, thus establishing their relevance.

1. Lewis, Carson, and others

Lewis's contention is that *storge, philia*, and *eros* are all "natural" loves, whereas *agape* alone is "gift-love" which is the kind of love that God is, and that he imparts to believers who may then manifest it to others. However, Lewis, along with other scholars of this persuasion, grants that the three "natural" loves can come to be infused with the spirit of *agape*, interpreted as selflessness, or willed self-sacrifice for the good of another. This approach, however, has come under strong criticism in recent decades. It arises from the study of individual words, without recognizing the large changes in the meaning of words during the period when the New Testament was written. Among the biblical writers, for example, there are times when *agape* and *philia* seem to be used interchangeably, and there are other times, both in the New Testament and the Septuagint, when the *agapao* group of words describes actions which are anything but selfless! On the other hand, when John 21:15–17 is examined, it seems, at least in that context, that *agape* represents a higher form of love than *philia*. These issues are spelled out cogently and in precise detail by D.A. Carson in *The Difficult Doctrine of the Love of God*. While the friendship implied in *philia* requires mutual reciprocation, *agape* can spring from the heart of one, whether or not there is a corresponding response from the other; though it is also true that the one manifesting *agape* longs for the response of the one who is loved.

2. Elliott on feeling

Matthew Elliott, in his book *Faithful Feelings: Emotion in the New Testament*, has tackled love from a different angle, re-establishing the emotions of God and those of his people as both real and significant. This was in response to a tendency, in many expositors, to play down the godly significance or positive contribution of emotion. Such tendency even invaded the understanding of *agape*, seen *as a response solely of the will*. It tended to empty passages of their genuine feeling as in the case when Mark records that Jesus looked at the rich young man *and loved him* (the verb *agapao* is used); or in the cases when John refers to himself as the disciple *whom Jesus loved* (*agapao* once again).

C. HOW, THEN, IS LOVE TO BE DISCERNED?

Our search for the *origin* of love is relatively straightforward. In the fourth chapter of John's first letter, the statement is made twice that God is love (4:8 and 4:16b); that is, that the being and nature of God can be summed up as *agape*. In the same letter, however, John's spiritual logic sees *important links between agape and other qualities* which themselves bend back, both to give extended clarity to love, and also to point to its practical application.

1. Knowledge, command, penetration

> This is how we know what love is: Jesus Christ laid down his life for us. And we ought to lay down our lives for one another. (1 John 3:16)

The beginning of love, then, involves *knowledge*—along with appreciation and gratitude—of something that exists. It is a form of awareness in which something is noticed and felt, rather than being recorded in a way that is purely cerebral or scientific. Here lies a complication, however. Many ethicists have perceived a gap between merely knowing and feeling about something on the one hand, and being obliged to act in the light of it, on the other. This is the puzzle as to how the "is" turns into an "ought." How is it that because we *know* Jesus laid down his life for us, we *ought* to do similarly for our brothers and sisters?

> And this is his command: to believe in the name of his Son, Jesus Christ, and to love one another as he commanded us.
> [a reference to personal faith in Christ, followed by a restatement of the "ought"]
> Those who keep his commands live in him, and he in them. And this is how we know that he lives in us: We know it by the Spirit he gave us. (1 John 3: 23,24)

The spiritual logic goes this way: trust in Jesus Christ opens a relationship with him whereby his love-nature penetrates our own, thus changing *our* nature, however gradually and partially, in the direction of his will. Thus, as his commands *become* ours, our obedience becomes willing and natural. And the one who carries out this transformation is the Holy Spirit gifted to believers through God's initiative in calling forth our faith. Overall then, John declares a link between love, on the one hand, and the reality of knowing God, obeying him, and maintaining a lively relationship with him through the ministry of the Spirit, on the other.

2. Lifestyle and truth

> Those who say, "I know him," [Jesus Christ] but do not do what he commands are liars, and the truth is not in them. But if anyone obeys his word, love for God is truly made complete in them. This is how we know we are in him: Whoever claims to live in him must live as Jesus did. (1 John 2:4,5)

The insight here is *about integrity*. One may claim a personal relationship with Christ, but if one's action—even allowing for the sin and failure in Christians, which John has anticipated earlier in his letter—runs regularly in a direction untypical of Christ's mind and lifestyle, the relationship claim has been shown to be false. Rather than completeness—that is, a progression in personal maturity—there is a hiatus between behavior and verbal profession.

For those who have eyes to see, love implies integrity between what one says and the way one acts. If this consonance is absent, it is seen to be an enacted lie: a departure from lived truth.

3. Perspective and priorities

> Do not love the world or anything in the world. If you love the world, love for the Father is not in you. For everything in the world—the cravings of sinful people, the lust of their eyes and their boasting about what they have and do—comes not from the Father but from the world. The world and its desires pass away, but whoever does the will of God lives forever. (1 John 2:15–17)

Let us note, in passing, that John sees as a distinct possibility that a person may love *(agapao)* what is abhorrent to God and opposed to his purposes. Manifestly, then, he has observed people who have made a

Love

commitment, whether consciously or in sub-conscious conformity with their society and culture, to a way of life which employs non-Christian values. These norms, though frequently most attractive, are transitory in the present, destructive in the lives of their devotees, and destined to disappear in the long-term. While conformity is central to an understanding of "the world" as John is using the term here, it denotes a total perspective out of alignment with God, and gives preference to priorities of the same kind.

Love, consequently, implies commitment of the whole person to whatever his or her "object-in-life" is; but John is pointing out, as Jesus did before him, that it is not possible to be devoted to two masters who are mutually opposed. He is calling upon his readers, and no doubt those with whom they would interact, *to choose* to respond to the love of the Father. Love, then, is to be linked with a realistic appraisal of spiritual alternatives, and the need for choice involving perspectives and priorities.

Love implies love not!

4. Upbuilding

Particularly in the thought of the apostle Paul, there occurs a goal of the upbuilding of other people.

> We who are strong *ought to bear with the failings of the weak* and not to please ourselves. We should all please our neighbors for their good, *to build them up.* (Romans 15:1, 2)

From the contexts where this idea is employed, it is the more experienced Christian who is to help in the upbuilding of the less experienced, the "parent" who is to provide for the upbuilding of the "children," the "shepherd" for the "flock." Within this process is a set of experiences which are valued because of their "building" qualities. One such is *understanding*, particularly in the preaching situation, where prophets ideally speak to people for their *strengthening, encouragement,* and *comfort*—all seen as ingredients of upbuilding (1 Corinthians 14:3–5). Others are *alertness, self-control,* and *the desire to live with Christ* (1 Thessalonians 5:6–11). Above all, however, the great factor in upbuilding is *love*. It is, indeed, "the most excellent way" (1 Corinthians 12:31b).

1 Corinthians 13 is, of course, Paul's great chapter on love, revealing crucial aspects of what it is, what it is not, as well as ways in which it contributes both to individual and to corporate upbuilding. There can be

ecstatic utterance or great eloquence, but without love these are little better than incoherent noise so far as person-building is concerned. Similarly there can be a display of gifted theorizing and extensive knowledge, but without love the upshot is negligible. Knowledge, indeed, held by someone who is concerned solely with his or her own interests, may give rise only to conceit, for it is only in association with love that knowledge builds up the one possessing it (1 Corinthians 8:1,2). Finally, the person with a loveless "faith," or the passionate, but loveless donor, or the self-sacrificing but loveless martyr will contribute nothing to the upbuilding of self or others.

5. Recognizing love

How, then, can genuine love be recognized in the hurly-burly of life, in either the first or the twenty-first century? Paul is not after an accurate theoretical formulation, but is pointing to actions and reactions that differentiate the loving person from one who is not. Love is patient: bearing with the boring, non-aggressive to the insulting, quietly challenging to the "know-all," polite to the persistent salesperson, kindly and gentle towards those who are physically or mentally vulnerable.

On the negative side, love is not self-preoccupied, and hence is not given to personal boastfulness or pride. Self is not the supreme priority, and hence there is no accumulation of grudges or of anger activated by memories from the past. Paul's command is, indeed, very pointed on this issue:

> ... if you have any encouragement from being united with Christ, if any comfort from his love, if any common sharing in the Spirit, if any tenderness and compassion, then make my joy complete by being like-minded, *having the same love*, being one in spirit and of one mind. Do nothing out of selfish ambition or vain conceit. *Rather, in humility value others above yourselves, not looking to your own interests but each of you to the interests of the others.* (Philippians 2:1–4)

And in this last sentence we discover a powerful ethical principle which expresses, although in somewhat different terms, the command to love one's neighbor as oneself. In Paul's formulation we need first to discern what *are* the interests of the others, i.e., the long-term good or benefit of the others, and then to find *ways of bringing these about*.

Finally, love delights in penetrating to the truth of any matter, and is protective where protection is needed. It loathes evil even when evil is associated with pleasure, economic gain, or the status granted to cultural conformity. Love has built into it hope and perseverance, even where the obstructions are heavy, and where a fruitful outcome can be reasonably expected only in future generations. And love is an investment in present fullness and maturity; and in ultimate perfection.

D. THE ATTITUDE OF LOVE

When a Christian engages in counseling, what attitude is presupposed? We have seen that friendliness *(philia)* is always appropriate, and that a commitment to playing our part in the coming interchange will have in mind the ultimate good of the client we are relating to *(agape)*. It sometimes happens that we find the client unattractive, or resistant, or avoidant, or extremely complicated. A concern for his or her interests will still be the dominant and underlying attitude of the counselor, who will bear with failings and weaknesses, and the frustrations imposed on well-made plans and schedules; and will be prepared, on the one hand, to bring strengthening, encouragement, and comfort. On the other hand, the client's initiatives and responses will sometimes be self-defeating and may require confrontation, reminders, or even correction. This will not be done out of personal irritation, but out of continuing care. Remuneration for counseling can also be a challenge to practical love. While the Australian Government has, and no doubt other administrations around the world have, in recent years, made some provision for mental health plans, including counseling, there will always be times when this is insufficient. Though it is a scriptural principle that the worker deserves their wages, the Christian counselor may at times need to provide for the client's best interests through fees that are self-sacrificial. From a Christian standpoint it is a scandal, in our contemporary world, for a human being to be denied counseling when it is clearly required.

E. CONCLUSION

What is desirable for a Christian counselor is a lifestyle continuously irrigated by the "living water" and satisfied by the "living bread" which are provided through a genuine relationship with Jesus Christ. Such a relationship will bring a transformation, usually gradual, though sometimes spluttering or faltering, that confers an overall integrity of thought, feeling, and action.

Walking Alongside

What is presupposed within a Christian perspective, then, is not only a process generating *love within the personality of the counselor*, reaching out to any person whatsoever who asks for help; but also a therapeutic process encouraging *love in counselees*, affecting and possibly transforming those life-relationships which had previously proved difficult for them.

In spite of this conclusion, someone may ask whether *the pursuit of happiness* should not be the ultimate target for a counselee, rather than love. Because of its prominence in the thinking of our culture, and, indeed, in the professional development of counselors, the issue is explored, in some detail, in the following chapter.

8

Happiness

My son-in-law and I once attended a concert in the Sydney Opera House, featuring Beethoven's Sixth Symphony. Each of the five movements received headings to describe *the feelings* that the composer wanted his listeners to experience. Here they are:

> Awakening of joyful feelings on arriving in the country
> Scene by the brook
> Merry gathering of country folk
> Thunderstorm
> Shepherd's Song: Happy and thankful feelings after the storm[1]

Through this magnificent composition we acknowledged Beethoven's power to evoke joyful feelings, merriment, and happiness. And we can use *happiness* as an umbrella term to cover joyfulness, merriment, and much more. But we cannot always summon Beethoven to our side when happiness is desired; when the thunderstorms of life have got us down. Indeed in many, many cases, men and women are driven into our counseling rooms because of their perceived *absence* of happiness.

From the revolutionary thinking of the late eighteenth century there emerged the ideal: The right to life, liberty, *and the pursuit of happiness.*

The same ideal, we can see, is alive and well at the beginning of the twenty-first century. At the fourth annual conference concerned with

---

1. *Sydney Symphony 2009 Season Great Classics,* 12.

Happiness and Its Causes, held in Sydney, Australia, the director referred to a statement made previously by the Dalai Lama in answer to the question: "What is the *purpose* of life?"

> His Holiness answered, "*the purpose of life is to seek happiness.*" [The director then continued]: "There is nothing more important. Happiness for oneself and others is the purpose of our life and everything that we can do to shed light on how one achieves happiness . . . can only be a good thing."[2]

The thought that emerges from a contemplation of Beethoven's genius is that life may be enriched by aesthetic experiences, drawn not only from music but from all forms of art; and that there will be those who devote their careers to such creativity to enhance our culture and our individual lives. But to say that life's *purpose* is to seek happiness, and that nothing is more important than this, is to raise some vital questions. The search for an understanding of happiness has continued both in ancient and modern times, and has certainly been given significant attention in the Scriptures of the Old and New Testaments.

A. WHAT IS HAPPINESS? A BIBLICAL VIEW

1. Blessedness

There is a variety of words both in the Old and New Testaments which indicate happiness, joy, enjoyment, and fulfillment. Some of them are virtually interchangeable with others, though the context can suggest minor differences. Some occur in partnership with other terms such as faith, hope, and grace, thus indicating that happiness or joy functions as part of an ideal Christian lifestyle, especially in the letters of Paul. And some take on special significance because of the object around which happiness or joy clusters. We start our exploration of this area by looking at the "beatitudes" found in Matthew 5 and Luke 6.

We note first that "the blessed," i.e., "the happy ones" *(makarioi)* are described in paradoxical terms: the mourners will be comforted, the meek will inherit, the hungry and thirsty will be filled. So, among other things, the values of the kingdom are displayed as "upside-down" when compared with contemporary values, in the past or the present. Being happy, then,

---

2. *Happiness and Its Causes: Official Conference Guide*, "From the Director", 2. My emphases.

cannot refer merely to pleasant internal feelings, but is inextricably linked with values—countercultural values—and the internalization of these as traits of character. Taking all this into account, *makarioi*, happy people, are those for whom congratulations are in order. They are fortunate and to be envied. Also their happiness has been *bequeathed*. There is someone who comforts, who causes them to inherit, who fulfils their hunger and thirst. Their happiness is *relational*.

2. Suffering within joy

We observe that this very kind of happiness can catch up *suffering* within its scope, as witness the extraordinary statement in Luke 6:22,

> Blessed are you when people hate you, when they exclude you and insult you and reject your name as evil, because of the Son of Man. *Rejoice in that day and leap for joy*, because great is your reward in heaven.

This emphasis is re-echoed by Paul in Romans 5, where a sequence in the personal development of the believer is traced from perseverance in suffering through to the end point of God pouring out his love into our hearts by the Holy Spirit. A strongly similar point is made in the letter of James, where the writer counsels:

> *Consider it pure joy*, my brothers and sisters, whenever you face trials of many kinds, because you know that the testing of your faith produces perseverance. Let perseverance finish its work so that you may be mature and complete, not lacking anything. (James 1:2)

3. Future and present joy

Crisscrossing with the theme of happiness-amidst-suffering, it is clear that the beatitudes have *an eschatological emphasis*; i.e., an emphasis on the coming kingdom and the standing of disciples within that future reign of God. However, as Matthew Elliott reminds us:

> The eschatological emphasis is important but we need to be careful that this is not allowed to rob joy of present emotion, which is also clear: we feel joy now because we believe things about the

future . . . Joy will not be complete until the coming age at which time it will come into fullness.[3]

The savor of the life that will be totally real in the future penetrates backwards, as it were, into the present, as a sweetening factor, though not one appreciated or embraced by all.

Where should we look for happiness?

A careful consideration of the beatitudes and the connected Scriptures referred to above will show that they are not generalized principles standing, as it were, with intrinsic force. The coming kingdom will be set up *by Christ*. Disciples will be insulted and excluded because they proclaim *the Son of Man*. What is tested is their faith in *their Lord*, and from this come perseverance, character, and hope. The beatitudes were part of the teachings of Jesus, but the gospel writers also draw attention to his life as a person, his death and resurrection as Redeemer, and the fact that he both lived and related joyfully, aiming also to bring this legacy of joy to his disciples.

We noted earlier that in the writings of Paul happiness or joy was frequently associated with faith, hope, and grace within an overall Christian lifestyle. In John's Gospel the strong association is between joy and obedience, friendship, and love. The emphasis is personal and relational. There is an interpenetration of love and joy among the Father, his Son Jesus, the disciple-friends and the Counselor-Spirit. Thus,

> As the Father has loved me, so have I loved you. Now remain in my love. If you keep my commands, you will remain in my love, just as I have kept my Father's commands and remain in his love. I have told you this *so that my joy may be in you and that your joy may be complete.* My command is this: Love each other as I have loved you. Greater love has no one than this: to lay down one's life for one's friends. You are my friends if you do what I command. (John 15:9–14)

As though to reinforce the connection between Jesus and joy, the writer to the Hebrews points to Jesus, not only as originator and finisher of faith, both individual and corporate, but also as exemplar. Having referred to the difficulties facing the particular group of believers in view, including the sin which distorts their progress, they are urged to persevere in pursuit of the goal that has been set for them. And then there follow the appropriate focus and clear sense of direction.

---

3. Elliott, *Faithful Feelings*, 171.

> ... let us run with perseverance the race marked out for us, fixing our eyes on Jesus, the pioneer and perfecter of faith. *For the joy set before him he endured the cross, scorning its shame,* and sat down at the right hand of the throne of God. Consider him who endured such opposition from sinners, so that you will not grow weary and lose heart. (Hebrews 12:1b–3)

We are pursuing a Christian answer to the question posed earlier: where should we look for happiness?

The new factor inserted into the human condition was a person, at once fully human and fully divine, *who lived in loving obedience to his Father, God, with whom the outcome was joy-in-relationship.* That person, Jesus, assured his disciples of *a similar outcome,* for them and those who would follow them, *if they came in loving obedience to himself:* that is, if they confessed "*Jesus is Lord.*" Knowing and trusting him would be joy in itself, both in untroubled times and also in times of adversity; but such joy would also be a pointer to the complete joy that Jesus foresaw for himself and for those who would contribute to the ethos of the coming Kingdom. In the meantime there would be happiness in any display, by the disciples, of the kingdom values played out in the contemporary world, however grotesque and provocative these might appear to those around.

When Christians look for happiness, then, they observe Jesus' joy, they share it through trusting and obeying him, and they willingly attempt a lifestyle which he spells out for them, however prevailing circumstances may affect them. In a word, *Jesus is their joy!*

In the seventeenth century, Johann Franck expressed this "word" in the form of a hymn:

> Jesus, priceless treasure,
> Source of purest pleasure,
> Truest friend to me;
> How my heart hath panted
> Till it well-nigh fainted,
> Thirsting, Lord, for Thee.
> Thine I am, O spotless Lamb,
> I will suffer nought to hide Thee,
> Nought I ask beside Thee.
>
> Hence all fears and sadness!
> For the Lord of gladness,
> Jesus, enters in;

> Those who love the Father,
> Though the storms may gather,
> Still have peace within;
> Yea, whate'er I here must bear,
> Still in Thee lies purest pleasure,
> Jesus, priceless treasure.[4]

B. What is happiness? A philosophical search

At the conference mentioned earlier, the *meaning* of happiness was not generally addressed. This is understandable, on the grounds that everyone really knows what happiness is, or, that it is so broad as to resist a clear-cut definition. The silence on this issue was, however, broken by a speaker in the field of neuroscience, who said he would be somewhat uneasy if happiness referred merely to *hedonism*. Instead, he preferred the term *eudaimonism*. This term was, in fact, used to describe happiness by several Greek philosophers, but particularly by Aristotle, in *The Nicomachean Ethics*.

1. Hedonism

Let us, however, deal with hedonism first. For some, "hedonism"—derived from a Greek word meaning "pleasure"—is nothing more nor less than indulgence in sensual pleasures; and there are very few thoughtful writers who would want to equate such pleasures with happiness. Certainly, Aristotle would not want to do so. His view was spelled out as follows:

> Pleasure is not the supreme good, and . . . not every pleasure is to be desired; . . . There do exist certain pleasures which are in themselves desirable, these being *distinguishable from the baser pleasures* by their specific qualities and the nature of their sources.[5]

Jesus' attitude was also clear on this. Thus his Parable of the Rich Fool:

> The ground of a certain rich man yielded an abundant harvest. He thought to himself, "What shall I do? I have no place to store my crops." Then he said, "This is what I'll do. I will tear down my barns and build bigger ones, and there I will store my surplus grain. And I'll say to myself, 'You have plenty of grain laid up for many years.

---

4. Franck, *The Baptist Hymn Book*, 851.
5. Aristotle, *The Nichomachean Ethics*, 293. My emphases.

Take life easy; eat, drink and be merry.'" But God said to him, "You fool! This very night your life will be demanded from you. Then who will get what you have prepared for yourself? This is how it will be with those who store up things for themselves but are not rich toward God." (Luke 12:16–21)

For others, however, hedonism is a theory wherein the good is *pleasure and the avoidance of pain,* without the implication of indulgence in *sensual* pleasures. R.H. Dotterer illustrates the point by reference to a philosopher who adopted this more moderate view:

> Following the example of Epicurus, . . . the egoistic hedonist prefers barley bread and water to richer fare; for he is persuaded that he will in this way gain the greatest amount of pleasure and the least amount of pain. He believes too that the satisfactions derived from social intercourse—poetry, painting, music, etc.—are better, because in the long-run safer.[6]

We presume that the neuroscience expert, referred to in chapter 6, was unwilling to equate happiness either with the cruder or the more sophisticated version of hedonism, because of his approving reference to *eudaimonia,* to which we now turn.

2. Eudaimonia

Foreshadowing the opinion of the Dalai Lama, and the ideal entrenched in the Constitution of the USA, Aristotle claimed, "Happiness we regard as the end to be sought in human life."[7]

However, this statement relies, for its power, on the ways in which happiness is spelled out, and Aristotle is at great pains to include a number of issues within its scope. First:

> It is . . . *intellectual activity* which forms perfect happiness for a man [sic]. We shall conclude that the life of the intellect is the best and pleasantest for man because the intellect more than anything else *is* the man. Thus it will be the happiest life as well.[8]

We note, incidentally, that intellectual activity is frequently equated, by Aristotle, with contemplation, speculation, and intelligence. In addition,

---

6. Dotterer, *Philosophy by Way of the Sciences,* 389.
7. Aristotle, *The Nichomachean Ethics,* 300.
8. Ibid., 304–5. My emphases.

> The moral as distinct from the intellectual life will, *though only in a secondary degree*, be happy too. Some [moral activities] . . . are actually the products of our bodily constitution—goodness of character is felt to have in many ways *an intimate connexion with the passions.*[9]

The point here is that Aristotle regarded the passions as being unruly and needing to be controlled. Hence goodness of character, for the reason given above, is not held to be purely intellectual. However, it is significant, even though morality takes second place where the causes of happiness are in view, that it is given *some* status. As we shall see later in this chapter, a contemporary quest for happiness, emerging in the late 1990s, has also included morality and goodness of character as worth examining.

Second, Aristotle links the happy life to *our make-up as human beings*. We have already seen that intellect predominantly constitutes the person. Now this is spelled out in semi-religious terms:

> Such a life will be too high for *human* attainment. It will not be lived by us in our merely human capacity but in virtue of something divine within us, and so far as this divine particle is superior to man's composite nature, to that extent will its activity be superior to that of other forms of excellence. If the intellect is divine compared with man, the life of the intellect must be divine compared with the life of a human creature. And we ought not to listen to those who counsel us *O man, think as man should and O mortal, remember your mortality.* Rather ought we, so far as in us lies, to put on immortality and to leave nothing unattempted in the effort to live in conformity with the highest thing within us. Small in bulk it may be, yet in power and preciousness it transcends all the rest. We may in fact believe that this is the true self of the individual, being the sovereign and better part of him.[10]

We note from this that the intellect is divine, that there is "a divine particle" within us which is the individual's "true self," and that we should live "in conformity" with this part of us in view of "its sovereignty." Now that Aristotle's "eudaimonism" has been unpacked, we may return to his original conviction—"happiness we regard as the end to be sought in human life"—and see it somewhat differently from the way we did initially. There is surely here an element of intellectual elitism which, incidentally,

9. Ibid., 305–6. My emphases.
10. Ibid., 305–6.

has had a marked influence throughout the centuries on the thought of the West. There is also a theory of the structure of personhood which, on the current scene, must be seen as highly debatable; and—intimately connected with this—there is the requirement to live in conformity with an inner voice, which is hard to define, and probably even harder to obey.

3. How do Aristotelian and Christian happiness match up?

There are words and phrases within Aristotle's statements that may sound vaguely familiar to some biblical statements. But, as one indicator, never in the Christian Scriptures is intellect, *per se*, considered divine. A statement from Paul's First Letter to the Corinthians makes the point.

> . . . it is written: "I will destroy the wisdom of the wise; the intelligence of the intelligent I will frustrate." [From Isaiah 29:14] Where are the wise? Where is the teacher of the law? Where is the philosopher of this age? Has not God made foolish the wisdom of the world? For since in the wisdom of God the world through its wisdom did not know him, God was pleased through the foolishness of what was preached to save those who believe. (1 Cor 1:19–21)

Having put forth the wise, the scholars, and the philosophers of his age as examples of "the intelligent," Paul claimed that, in spite of these socially honored gifts, the ultimately worthwhile thing—to know God—had not eventuated. What had seemed to be foolish in the eyes of the intelligentsia had, however, been effective in helping people to know, and along with that, to trust God. It is true, of course, that in the Wisdom Literature, wisdom is sometimes personified as a woman, brought forth as "the first of Yahweh's works" (Proverbs 8:22), and of whom it is claimed that "those who find me find life and receive favor from the LORD" (Proverbs 8:35). But whether such references are regarded as pre-Christian intimations of God, or a poetical rendering of God's nature, the constant refrain in this literature (Proverbs 9:10, for example) is: "The fear of the LORD is the beginning of wisdom, and knowledge of the Holy One is understanding"; and knowing and trusting God in awe and humility is what "the fear of the LORD" is all about.

As another indicator of Aristotle's seemingly biblical language, he spoke, as mentioned above, about "something divine within us" naming this "a divine particle" and "the true self of the individual." In our earlier chapter entitled *People*, we emphasized that the Bible constantly sees people as whole beings, rather than an assemblage of parts—or "particles." We now add that anything "divine within us" is granted *relationally* when "the Spirit himself testifies *with our spirit*, [our responsiveness as whole and trusting persons] that we are God's children" (Romans 8:16). That there is "a true self" can be agreed, as noted earlier, this being the deep "core" or "heart" that is organized and developed about whomever or whatever the person holds as an object of worship. But this is a concept far distant from Aristotle's "self" which is essentially intellectual.

4. Other philosophical approaches

There are now, of course, numerous other approaches to the question: what is happiness? Many of these have built upon the questions raised in Ancient Greece, while new issues have appeared in the light of changed circumstances and cultures. It would be impossible to deal with these in the remainder of this chapter. One, however, needs to be named because of its considerable influence, and this is the position of Utilitarianism, espoused by philosophers such as Jeremy Bentham and John Stuart Mill, who formulated and extended an ethical theory, containing the criterion: *the greatest happiness of the greatest number*. The criticisms of this position have been numerous, including its dubious treatment of justice and the fact that it is impossible to quantify the result of the criterion. Overall, we must conclude that happiness, as dealt with in philosophy, is difficult to define, and therefore to attain. In spite of these problems, many factors have been shown to be relevant, and without doubt the search will continue.

C. WHAT IS HAPPINESS? THE APPROACH OF TIBETAN BUDDHISM

"The purpose of life is to seek happiness." This quotation was given earlier in the chapter as a considered statement by the fourteenth Dalai Lama, Tenzin Gyatso. Enthroned just before he turned five, he began to exercise leadership in both religious and political matters when only sixteen! After attempting to negotiate a peaceful agreement with the invading Chinese, he finally concluded that this was useless, and made his escape to India in 1959, along with thousands of Tibetan refugees. In 1987, after careful thought, he proposed a plan to the Chinese leadership whereby each side would concede certain rights, but would negotiate a reasonable peace. The

Chinese would have none of it, but the international community was so impressed that two years later he received the Nobel Peace Prize. Since that time, Tibetan Buddhism, with the Dalai Lama as its chief spokesman, has made a considerable impact on the Western world, where his contribution has been broadened to encompass the promotion of human rights generally. As in the case of a very similar statement on happiness, given by Aristotle, where it was crucial to discover the issues lying beneath the statement, so it is no less important to investigate such issues in this case.

There are many varieties of Buddhism, and Tibetan Buddhism is aligned with "The Great Vehicle" or Mahayana tradition, as distinct from the Hinayana tradition, which the Mahayana followers derisively call "The Lesser Vehicle." The Hinayanists claim to have the authentic teachings of Sakyamuni, (or Siddhartha Gautama) the historic Buddha, and therefore claim to have the pure form of Buddhism. They also avoid any place for gods in their system. Tibetan Buddhism does, however, find a place for gods and godlike creatures. Even within their account of transmigrations, bad action—i.e., bad karma—may give rise to a new life as an animal, hungry ghost, or hell-being; while good karma may result in a new human being, a demi-god, or a god.

1. A world view

John Powers, author of *Introduction to Tibetan Buddhism*, decided that the focus of his study would be on

> what Tibetans believe the Buddha to have taught, and not on what modern historians would accept as authentic teachings. Among the most basic and pervasive of these are teachings attributed to Buddha concerning karma and rebirth . . . according to Tibetan Buddhists, Buddha taught that one's present life is only one in a beginningless series of rebirths, and each of these is determined by one's actions in previous lives. These actions are collectively referred to as "karma."[11]

From these fundamental teachings, the conclusion is drawn that suffering is the great problem facing human beings. The cycle of rebirths is seen as a helpless transmigration within which beings are trapped, and which is actively perpetuated by ignorance. Ignorance is seen as a *cognitive*

---

11. Powers, *Introduction to Tibetan Buddhism*, 54.

problem, and hence its solution must tackle the task of a *cognitive rearrangement* of world view, both at the individual and corporate levels. [*Comment*: On this particular issue, there is a similarity of approach to that of both Cognitive Therapy and Cognitive Behavioral Therapy on the contemporary counseling scene, where the client's cognitive beliefs are challenged. In all cases, of course, the criteria for something to be accepted as true remains a major issue.]

According to Powers,

> The first requirement is the development of dissatisfaction with cyclic existence. As long as one is basically comfortable within cyclic existence, there is no possibility of release. One must develop a profound revulsion, looking back on one's beginningless births with disgust and vowing to break the cycle by any means necessary . . . Next, one must emulate Buddha's example and develop the positive moral qualities that he cultivated. This leads to mental peace and equanimity, which are necessary to successful meditation. Meditation is the key to overcoming ignorance, for through meditation one can develop insight into the true nature of reality, which acts as a counteragent to ignorance. Successful development of insight allows one to transcend the influence of karma, to end the ignorant engagement in actions that bind one to continued transmigration, and eventually to end the cycle altogether.[12]

2. Elimination of "thirst" and "self"

In the course of this development there are at least two kinds of things which have to be eliminated. The first of these is *desire* or *thirst*. Desire presents itself in three forms: desire for pleasure, desire for continued existence, and desire for non-existence. Each of these must be discarded. If there is no desire, then there is no suffering connected with its non-fulfillment. Says Powers,

> Buddhist philosophy holds that all three kinds of desire are mistaken and that all must be overcome *in order to find lasting happiness*.[13]

In our account of Buddhist thinking thus far, this is the first mention of happiness, and it should be noted that this is conditional upon a highly

---

12. Ibid., 55-6.
13. Ibid., 58. My emphases.

disciplined state of mind where, among other things, a large area of motivation has ceased to exist.

The second thing needing to be eliminated is the idea, within a human being, of *a self*. Before proceeding, however, with a fuller explanation of this, one further Buddhist belief must be recognized because of its penetrating significance in the total Buddhist structure. It is believed that *nothing is permanent*, and that all things change continuously. This view was also held by the Greek philosopher Heraclitus, and was reflected, in the twentieth century, in the philosophical and educational writings of John Dewey.

Continuing now with the discussion of "the self," Powers records what the Buddhist texts say on this issue:

> The basis for the imputation of self is the collection of elements that together constitute the psycho-physical personality, which Buddhism divides into five "aggregates" . . . (1) form, (2) feelings, (3) discriminations, (4) compositional factors, and (5) consciousness . . . Taken together, they are the constituents of the individual, but we mistakenly impute something more, an essence, a self, or soul. When one analyzes this concept to locate its basis, however, all that one finds are these five aggregates, none of which can constitute a self because they are constantly changing, whereas the self that sentient beings imagine, is self-sufficient and enduring.[14]

However we judge the adequacy of this analysis, the argument, just recorded, is a clear-cut case of *reductionism*. Interestingly, at its end-point, it is similar to the conclusions of some postmodernists who wish to "deconstruct" the individual person, so that there is no recognition of "a self."

But now, to continue the quotation commenced above:

> Since the innate idea of self implies an autonomous, unchanging essence, if such a thing were in fact the core of one's being, it would mean that change would be impossible, and one would be stuck being just what one is right now. Because there is no such self, however, we are constantly changing, and thus are open toward the future. One's nature is never fixed and determined, and so through engaging in Buddhist practice one can exert control over the process of change and progress in wisdom, compassion, patience, and other good qualities. One can even become a buddha, a fully enlightened being who is completely liberated from all frailties, sufferings, and limitations of ordinary beings. But this is only

14. Ibid., 62.

> possible because there is no fixed and static self, no soul that exists self-sufficiently, separated from the ongoing process of change.[15]

3. The path of meditation

Our quest at this point, as earlier, is to discover where happiness fits within the overall schema of Buddhist doctrine and practice. As before, Powers contributes to this issue in an informed way.

> It should be noted that Buddhism does not deny the presence of happiness in human life. What it does deny is that happiness can be permanent for those enmeshed in cyclic existence, which is characterized by constant change. Even when one finds happiness, it must inevitably end, only to be replaced by loss, longing, and unhappiness. This state of affairs is considered to be unacceptable, and Buddhism teaches a path by which this unsatisfactory situation may be transcended.[16]

Presumably, then, when the Dalai Lama said, "The purpose of life is to seek happiness," he was referring, not to some transient state which will eventually be replaced, but to the end point of the total Buddhist path, achieved in large part by the advanced stages of meditation. But even here, further questions arise.

Within the complexities of Buddhist meditation, the "Four Concentrations" appear to play an important role. And once again we call on Powers' account.

> One reaches the first concentration by overcoming the subtlest levels of attachment to the Desire Realm, the lowest level of cyclic existence and the one in which we exist ... By successfully attaining it, the meditator can achieve rebirth in this state, which is said to be endowed *with joy and bliss*. To reach the other three concentrations, the procedure is similar: The meditator views the lower concentration as gross and the higher one as subtle and seeks to attain it.
> In the first two concentrations *joy and bliss are present,* but in the third concentration *joy is absent but bliss is present.* One also develops *meditative equanimity* in the third concentration, which is strengthened in the fourth concentration to the point where bliss

---

15. Ibid., 65.
16. Ibid., 56.

also disappears and is replaced with a *pervasive equanimity*. The reason why joy and bliss are progressively eliminated is that they interfere with mental stability.[17]

What we are faced with now is a set of distinctions among happiness, joy, bliss, and equanimity. There is just the chance, of course, that this is purely verbal: that we are arguing merely about words. There is the further difficulty of translating adequately the convictions of a complex Eastern worldview into the terms of Western understanding. Having accepted these limitations, however, we may be forgiven for asking precisely what the Dalai Lama was referring to when he claimed that the purpose of life was to seek *happiness*. It could scarcely be the happiness which, in the end, is followed by loss, longing, and unhappiness. Nor could it be joy or bliss, both of which must be replaced in the end. What is left is *equanimity*. This word is said to mean: *evenness of mind or temper; calmness; composure*.[18] Granted, perhaps, that the purpose of life may be to seek equanimity, is this what a Western audience would have discerned when hearing the word "happiness"?

And so, in this very brief exploration of Christianity, Western philosophers, and Tibetan Buddhism, the mention of "happiness" requires us to avoid the shallows of popular generalizations and to be prepared, instead, to go deeper, until we discern the undercurrents that may propel us either into a broad consensus, or, as we have tended to imply, into a variety of quite distinct and different directions.

D. WHERE DO WE NOW LOOK FOR CHARACTER CRAFTED FROM MORALITY?

1. The Seligman route

For the greater part of the twentieth century Western psychology had been loath to include on its agenda the question of human character. Personality had been studied in considerable detail, but character, which carried moral overtones, was felt to be outside the area of empirical theory and measurement. In 1998, the prestigious Martin Seligman became president of the American Psychological Association and used his presidential address to oppose the trend away from the study of character and to propose

17. Ibid., 72–3. My emphases.
18. *The Macquarie Dictionary*, 588.

the innovative concept of *Positive Psychology*. He developed the idea of *character strengths*, derived from recognized virtues, and argued that these could be measured in much the same way as personality traits. He was clear, however, that such strengths were not to be identified according to whether they yielded tangible outcomes or not, i.e., whether they were part of a causal chain. Instead, character strengths would be recognized because they were *morally* valued; recognized by their intrinsic worth. Any tangible benefit would, then, be a kind of bonus, even though it may possibly have been anticipated. The sizeable and comprehensive book that expressed this new turn-of-the-century emphasis in psychology was authored by Christopher Peterson and Martin E.P. Seligman, and was entitled *Character Strengths and Virtues: A Handbook and Classification*. It is at this point that we encounter, once again, the idea of *happiness*.

Within the Seligman project, "happiness" is equated with "subjective well-being,"[19] and is viewed as *an outcome*, not as an ultimate goal nor as *the purpose of life*. "The [morally] good life, for oneself and for others" is the strength lying behind subjective well-being, as well as many other outcomes.[20] In other words *the happy life* has been caught up within the ambit of *the morally good life*. Character is to be pursued; happiness is likely to happen! And at this point in the chapter, we turn our attention to values and character.

There was a second kind of motivation, however, behind the eruption of Positive Psychology. Due to a range of factors, including the latest version of the respected *Diagnostic and Statistical Manual of Mental Disorders (DSM)*, sponsored by the American Psychiatric Association (1994) and the *International Classification of Diseases (ICD)*, sponsored by the World Health Organization (1990)—both of which concerned themselves with accurately delineating patterns of psychological pathology—the balance in psychology was judged, by Seligman and others, to have overemphasized what was difficult or weak in human beings. Peterson and Seligman's disquiet is expressed as follows:

> Nothing comparable to the DSM or ICD exists for the good life. When psychiatrists and psychologists talk about mental health, wellness, or wellbeing, they mean little more than the absence of disease, distress, and disorder. It is as if falling short of diagnostic criteria should be the goal for which we should all strive . . .

19. Peterson and Seligman, *Character Strengths and Virtues*, 19.
20. Ibid., 17.

> This handbook focuses on what is right about people and specifically about the strengths of character that make the good life possible. We follow the example of the DSM and ICD . . . by proposing a classification scheme and by devising assessment strategies for each of its entries. The crucial difference is that the domain of concern for us is not psychological illness but psychological health.[21]

The authors freely acknowledge the work of those in the twentieth century who *did* give attention to psychological wellbeing, but they have now embarked, in a systematic way, on bringing about a positive counterbalance in psychology. Their strategy for doing this entails a return to the recognition of character, as described above.

While we would commend such a project, there are some issues to be faced. First, the work required to bring it about would seem immense. In brief, it would require that psychology should at this point take, as its spouse, the field of moral philosophy, developed throughout the ages. It would not be sufficient to have one or other subservient or merely contributory. Second, the core concerns of both disciplines would need to be dealt with at full stretch; sticking points and new territory being worked through with the rigor and debate historically attached to both domains. Were this done, there could be an interesting connection between this merged endeavor and the field of biblical anthropology which, though not incorporating a worldwide record of cultures and ethics, is intrinsically concerned with human beings, individual and corporate, along with their relationships and moral values. In particular, biblical anthropology contributes the concept of *shalom*, mentioned in chapter 4, which draws attention to *human flourishing*, inclusive both of its psychological and moral aspects. *Shalom* subsumes concepts of health, *but also gives them practical meaning through the way it conceives an overall pattern of relationships.*

At this very early stage of the Seligman route, James P. Gubbins has penned a brief but penetrating critique of the Peterson and Seligman book which is generally appreciative but which also draws attention to some weaknesses and omissions. We shall, however, postpone noting his salient points until a little later.

---

21. Ibid., 4.

2. The Lewis route

In the meantime we draw attention to a little book, sixty-four pages in length and published in 1947, by the remarkable and influential Christian writer, C.S. Lewis: *The Abolition of Man*. Although the book is a critique of a school text-book on English—which, of course, was Lewis's professional field—its broader significance lies in its championing of the existence of universal values which can be declared "true," and which, in their collective form, he calls "the Way" or "the Tao." According to Lewis:

> This conception in all its forms, Platonic, Aristotelian, Stoic, Christian, and Oriental alike, I shall henceforth refer to for brevity simply as "the Tao". Some of the accounts of it which I have quoted will seem, perhaps, to many of you merely quaint or even magical. But what is common to them all is something we cannot neglect. It is the doctrine of objective value, the belief that certain attitudes are really true, and others really false, to the kind of thing the universe is and the kind of things we are.[22]

Lewis thus anticipated Seligman's task half a century before the advent of Positive Psychology, at least so far as the values which are basic to character are concerned. In the nine pages of the appendix, which he modestly called "Illustrations of the *TAO*," he classifies particular values under the heading of general laws. These values come, not only from the traditions and individuals mentioned above, but also from Ancient Egyptian, Old Norse, Babylonian, Hindu, Greek, Roman, Red Indian, Anglo-Saxon, and Australian Aboriginal sources. His grasp of some of the languages and most of the cultures was prodigious and, of course, there is an integrative value when all the data are held and processed in the mind of one person. His version of the general moral laws is as follows:

> The Law of General Beneficence
> The Law of Special Beneficence
> Duties to Parents, Elders, Ancestors
> Duties to Children and Posterity
> The Law of Justice
> The Law of Good Faith and Veracity
> The Law of Mercy
> The Law of Magnanimity[23]

---

22. Lewis, *The Abolition of Man*, 17.
23. Ibid., 56–64.

3. The Wallace-Havel-Hill route

Three Western Australians, all of them educationists, decided in the 1990s that they would explore the possibility of agreement on values among the three monotheistic communities within their state: the Jewish community, the Islamic community, and the Christian churches, both Catholic and Protestant. In a time of educational heart-searching, which has continued and which involves both Federal and State governments within Australia, these three people wanted to bring discourse on values into the general debate on state schooling. The goal would be to create a "Values Framework," which would be an infrastructure, as it were, for present attempts to construct or revise school curricula.[24]

A hard-working consortium finally agreed on a Values Framework in three sections:

1.0 Ultimate Values
2.0 Democratic Values
3.0 Educational Values

Each section in turn focused on four issues:

1. Life Perspectives
2. Perspectives on the Individual
3. Perspectives on Society
4. Perspectives on the Natural World

Up to seven agreed affirmations were listed in each of the appropriate columns.

It is clear that the consortium set out to explore *a restricted area of values* across a restricted number of faith communities who might be expected to have certain values in common; all within the educational area alone. Nevertheless their findings could well impinge on some areas of psychology and sociology, and would not be without relevance in the practice of counseling.

In terms of scope, the Western Australian study could be seen to lie at the *particular* end of a value investigation, and with curriculum construction in mind; as distinct from the more general and universal emphasis of C.S. Lewis. Lewis, on the other hand, was concerned *more generally* that school students should not have their characters distorted by an education that claimed to be value-free, but was subtly indoctrinative. The two emphases, however, are entirely compatible and each valuable in its own sphere.

---

24. Hill, "Mainstreaming Values Issues in Education," 7–16.

4. The Gubbins critical survey of the new Seligman highway

As indicated above, Gubbins finds much to commend and learn from in the Peterson and Seligman book. In the positive part of his critique, he cites a number of correlation studies where, for example, people with a disposition of gratitude show higher levels of vitality and optimism; forgiving people show less anxiety, depression, and hostility; and religiousness and spirituality make someone more likely to achieve any desired character strength. He also appreciates the commitment of the authors to cross-cultural research, and notes that Positive Psychology has been the forum for much new and valuable knowledge. This being said, Gubbins observes:

> The authors take their lead from Ninian Smart's *World Philosophies* in which Smart identifies China, South Asia, and the West as the three most influential cultures in human history. They then concentrate on the writings of Confucianism, Taoism, Hinduism, Buddhism, ancient Greek philosophy, Judaism, Christianity, and Islam . . . [but later] . . . discuss the other three major literary sources: catalogues of virtue, modern psychology, and philosophy.

[We may well note the broad similarity here to the list of cultures considered by C.S. Lewis, except that Lewis does not include modern psychology.]

> After studying the writings of these seven world religions and of Ancient Greece, abstracting lists of virtues, then comparing, analyzing, and condensing these lists, the authors conclude that they discern within each tradition and across the traditions six higher-order virtue categories:
>
> 1. Wisdom and knowledge
> 2. Courage
> 3. Humanity
> 4. Justice
> 5. Temperance
> 6. Transcendence[25]

[We observe that approximately half only of these categories coincide with Lewis's list.]

In addition to the six higher-order virtues, the authors discerned twenty-four "strengths of character," each of which was classified as belonging to one of the higher-order virtues.

---

25. Gubbins, "Positive Psychology," 184.

With this outline in place, Gubbins commences his negative critique on Positive Psychology. Internally, he perceives that the character strengths are the important things to arise out of the cross-cultural investigation, and that the six virtues are "vague categories within which to throw the character strengths . . . The bulk of the volume is devoted to the character strengths, while little is devoted to the virtues".[26] The point arising from these observations is as follows:

> Even a cursory look at the virtues and their strengths makes evident the sometimes loose, sometimes ill-fitting relationships between the two. Why, for example, is integrity or honesty a strength of courage and not of justice or temperance? Why does the strength of forgiveness and mercy fall under the virtue of temperance and not humanity?[27]

Furthermore the actual naming of character strengths, according to Gubbins, draws directly, in the majority of cases, from empirical psychology and associated measurements.[28] All of this implies a bias towards the psychological ingredients in the purported multidisciplinary exercise.

As if to add fuel to his developing critical fire, Gubbins contends:

> Positive Psychology's six higher-order virtues do not correspond, despite the authors' claims, to the virtues found within or across the traditions of Confucianism, Taoism, Hinduism, Buddhism, ancient Greek philosophy, Judaism, Christianity, and Islam, [and] that other conceptualizations of virtues are more compelling—most notably those from philosophy and the world religions.[29]

Not content with this generalization, Gubbins illustrates his points with comparisons in the treatment of the virtues between Aquinas, Kierkegaard, and Jonathan Edwards, as prominent Christian contributors, on the one hand, and the findings of the Positive Psychology authors on the other. The present writer is in broad agreement with Gubbins' viewpoints, both positive and negative, but would add that where the Peterson and Seligman book touches upon Christianity, there tends to be a measure of distortion. For example:

---

26. Ibid., 191.
27. Ibid.
28. Ibid., 192.
29. Ibid., 193–4.

> Moral philosophy changed with the growing influence of Christianity, which saw God as the giver of laws by which one should live. Righteous conduct no longer stemmed from inner virtues but rather from obedience to the commandments of God. The guiding question therefore changed from inquiries about the traits of a good person to "What are the right things to do?"
>
> As Christianity waned in importance, divine law eventually gave way to a secular equivalent dubbed moral law, but the focus remained on specifying the rules of right conduct as opposed to strengths of character.[30]

The naiveté of this comment is quite remarkable! Even if its starting point is the giving of the Ten Commandments in the Old Testament—often held to be a specification of rules for conduct—there has been a complete neglect of the Jewish *shema*, as in Deuteronomy 6:4–6, which has always been *interpretive* of the Decalogue, given in chapter 5. Thus:

> Hear, O Israel: the LORD our God, the LORD is one. *Love* the LORD your God with all your heart and with all your soul and with all your strength. These commandments that I give you today are to be *on your hearts*.

The biblical emphasis then was clearly on a heartfelt love of God bringing about a willingness to identify with God's own revealed character: to be morally good and right. The biblical focus is not on the rules of right conduct *per se*, but on the character of God, from which we can distill guidelines for right conduct. In the New Testament, the connection between loving God the Son and reflecting his character in action is, if anything, clearer still. Towards the end of his ministry, and anticipating a final judgment, Jesus projected the following:

> ... the King will say to those on his right, "Come, you who are blessed by my Father; take your inheritance, the kingdom prepared for you since the creation of the world. For I was hungry and you gave me something to eat, I was thirsty and you gave me something to drink, I was a stranger and you invited me in, I needed clothes and you clothed me, I was sick and you looked after me, I was in prison and you came to visit me."
>
> Then the righteous will answer him, "Lord, when did we see you hungry and feed you, or thirsty and give you something to drink? When did we see you a stranger and invite you in, or needing

---

30. Peterson and Seligman, *Character Strengths and Virtues*, 10.

clothes and clothe you? When did we see you sick or in prison and go to visit you?"

The King will reply, "Truly I tell you, whatever you did for one of the least of these brothers and sisters of mine, you did *for me*." (Matthew 25:34–40)

5. What then, finally, of the Seligman route?

It is noble in conception. It has reclaimed, for psychological attention, the insight that moral character and characteristics are intrinsic to human behavior. It has collected and tested evidence that links virtuous attitudes and psychological outcomes. It has commended the search for a broad consensus, among the major religions and philosophies of human history, with respect to the existence of objective moral virtues and individual moral strengths. And it has restored an emphasis on the wellbeing of human beings, to balance the huge attention given by psychology in the twentieth century to human malfunctioning.

On the other hand, it does not seem to have comprehended the size of the territory to be explored. We included, in our display, the remarkable effort of C.S. Lewis in attempting to collect basic moral values from as many religious and philosophical sources as possible. Compared with the Seligman project, however, this was an endeavor with strict limits, and one that made no effort to link up systematically with modern psychology. Also included was the study, devised for educational purposes, of ultimate values, democratic values, and educational values, wherein consensus was achieved among three monotheistic religious groups. Once again, the limits were set strictly and deliberately for curriculum purposes. The point, made implicitly up till now, is that the psychological community may have much to gain from smaller forays into its newly expanded territory, while larger integrative efforts may need to pause for the time being.

To be more critical, the Seligman project, for reasons given cogently in the Gubbins critique, does not seem to have accepted the need for the suggested marriage between psychology and moral philosophy. So far as contributions from religions and moral philosophy are concerned, it seems that the externalities, the "headlines," were largely taken at face value, without a deeper exploration of their philosophical context. Added to this is a tendency, described in some detail above, to get some issues badly wrong through the lack of grasp of the theology behind a religious value, or the theory behind a philosophical ethic. To be blunt, in these areas the large project, as might have been predicted, has been superficial. And when one needs to find categories to fill important gaps in an important story, one will naturally turn to the resources with which one is most familiar; in this case, psychology. One further point is that when the new endeavor is called *Positive* Psychology, emphasizing wellbeing, the reaction in the public sphere, and particularly in the counseling sphere, will be to equate the new emphasis with *happiness*.

E. CONCLUSION AND TRANSITION

We have hopefully demonstrated in this chapter that "happiness" can only be clarified when seen in the context of a surrounding theory or world view, and thus that it will have different or even contradictory meanings in the mouths of various prophets at particular moments in time. *Happiness is a by-product that emerges in the pursuit of an ultimately worthwhile goal. It is not, in itself, such a goal.*

In recent therapeutic literature, especially when applied to counseling, there has been a considerable emphasis on "*mindfulness.*" In the structure of the present book we include it now, immediately after the chapter on "*happiness*," because the two notions appear to have a certain amount in common. Those who commend mindfulness tend to see it as an attitude towards living through which one gains "*peace of mind*," and this seems to place it at least within the same family—perhaps a sibling or cousin—of happiness. One of the emphases, though by no means the only one, in the Old and New Testaments, is what I have named "inwardness." Though, in the scriptural account, inward experience is one end of a dimension of which the other end is responsible action, it has its own set of recognizable facets. We now juxtapose inwardness with mindfulness.

9

Inwardness

We human beings exist in a constantly changing environment for the most part, and in a disordered social fabric throughout most of our world. This cannot but be reflected in thought, feelings, values, attitudes, and judgments. Of course, as the rate of change accelerates, there must be significant changes in outward behavior and action, both individual and corporate, but there will be equally significant shifts in the pattern of individual inwardness.

A. LOOKING BACK

In the history of modern psychology, among the early significant trends was an interest in introspection. This strand of psychological enquiry had developed rather exacting routines to ensure that inward experience, in spite of its acknowledged fuzziness, could be dealt with systematically and in recognizable categories. Revolution, however, began to surface in the form of a science of psychology concentrating solely and objectively on outward behavior which, in principle, was measurable; and need not take into consideration experiences which were, by their very nature, hard to discern and describe. Thus, in the period immediately before and during World War I, Behaviorism took the stage and Introspectionism died a natural death.

Walking Alongside

Over the years, strict Watsonian Behaviorism became modified, and was increasingly linked with an emphasis on cognitive aspects of human activity, which at the time amounted to one small step in the direction inwards, so far as understanding personal experience was concerned. While the study of moods and emotions would require even more extensive empirical observation, at least a Cognitive–Behavioral approach promised a measure of control with therapeutic benefits, especially in the treatment of depression, though not restricted to that area. (It goes without saying, of course, that numerous other aspects of psychology and counseling were being pursued at the same time as the sequences noted here.)

Almost suddenly, about seventy years after the Behaviorist Revolution, many groups of people, tiring of the persistent noise without, and aware of the cluttering of their minds within, made a decisive turn—an ancient one, as it happens—and sought *silence*; yes, "empty" silence for some few groups, but "silence" inhabited by individual ideas and ceaseless "self-talk" for most. This "stream of consciousness," known to us all, may at times be seen as a harbinger of creativity; and many writers of books and planners of strategies would testify to the relevance, and happy intrusiveness, of words that were not invited but nevertheless made speed in the mind. But the same self-talk can also be seen as a terrible distraction from what is worthwhile, requiring *the discipline of attention* to open the mind to a variety of new experiences—some of them therapeutic.

Curiously, at the same time, a set of new technologies had conspired to allow the observation of brain functioning with a directness and detail never imagined before. This new area of enquiry and research has been called *neuroscience* as mentioned earlier. Neuroscience had now revealed the fact that environmental experiences could, indeed, affect the shape and the functioning of the brain itself, along with related experiential states.

In the late twentieth century, then, there was a renewed interest in inwardness or inner experience, described in verbal experiential terms; and there was a new science available, which bade fair to describe the same experience in terms of objective findings. Hence the theoretical possibilities that hypotheses developed from personal inner experience could be checked and modified by scientific brain observation; and that hypotheses suggested by observing brain states could be tested or expanded through correlating these with appropriate subjective findings. Later in this chapter we shall draw attention to Daniel Siegel's work, which tackles these possibilities in a ground-breaking way. In the meantime we shall begin to

B. INWARDNESS IN THE BIBLE

In earlier chapters, a number of issues were introduced which now appear important when linked with inwardness.

1. Insights about people

When dealing with Old Testament person-words, it was noted that *leb* and *ruach* presented a view of the person as *oriented*, formed largely, indeed, by whatever is the *focus* of affection in his or her life. Related to this, the terms frequently referred to the center of one's being, i.e., with *the core self or heart.* Usage in the New Testament confirmed a broadly parallel view where the words *nous* and *kardia* were considered.

2. Insights about providence

What was traced out in detail in chapter 5, largely from the Psalms, was that God not only created and provided for his creatures, but also took steps to *communicate* with them in a variety of ways. God is mindful of his created beings, and cares for them. God "looks down and sees all humankind; from his dwelling place he *watches* all who live on earth—he who forms the hearts of all, who considers everything they do."[1] In addition, however, *God probes the minds and hearts of all people.* This process, initiated by God, suggests a penetrating interaction with individuals at an inward personal level. Hence also John commences his Gospel by proclaiming that Jesus, himself the Word or Message, was the true light that gives "light" *to every person.*

3. Insights about participation

Recollecting the research carried out by Hubble and associates, traced out in chapter 1, we focus on one of the major streams said to be involved in successful therapy, and also to be common to all instances of such therapy. To quote Hubble once again,

1. Psalm 33:13–15.

> These factors are part of the client or the client's life circumstances that aid in recovery despite the client's formal participation in therapy. They consist of the client's strengths, supportive elements in the environment, and even in chance events. In short, they are what clients bring to the therapy room and what influences their lives outside. As examples of these factors, persistence, faith, a supportive grandmother, membership in a religious community, sense of personal responsibility, a new job, a good day at the tracks, a crisis successfully managed; all may be included.[2]

What clients bring to the therapy room may include many things, as illustrated above, but would helpfully include snippets of that persistent inward conversation, in which there are times when God is searching and challenging and inviting, but with differing kinds of response in different people at different stages of their growth. The Christian counselor can become ever more alert to clues on what the client reveals, especially where the whole process has been surrounded by prayer. Jesus' parable of the sower gives some direct insights on the dynamics involved in hearing and doing. Here is Eugene Peterson's paraphrase of Matthew 13:1–13; 18–23.

> A Harvest Story
> Jesus left the house and sat on the beach. In no time at all a crowd gathered along the shoreline, forcing him to get into a boat. Using the boat as a pulpit, he addressed his congregation, telling stories.
> "What do you make of this? A farmer planted seed. As he scattered the seed some of it fell on the road, and birds ate it. Some fell in the gravel; it sprouted quickly but didn't put down roots, so when the sun came up, it was strangled by the weeds. Some fell on good earth, and produced a harvest beyond his wildest dreams."
> "Are you listening to this? Really listening?"
>
> *Why Tell Stories?*
> The disciples came up and asked, "Why do you tell stories?"
> He replied, "You've been given insight into God's kingdom. You know how it works. Not everybody has this gift, this insight; it hasn't been given to them. Whenever someone has a ready heart for this, the insights and understandings flow freely. But if there is no readiness, any trace of receptivity soon disappears. That's why I tell stories: to create readiness, to nudge the people toward receptive insight. In their present state they can stare till doomsday and not see it, listen till they're blue in the face and not get it.

---

2. Hubble et al., *The Heart & Soul of Change*, 9.

The Meaning of the Harvest Story
"Study this story of the farmer planting seed. When anyone hears news of the kingdom and doesn't take it in, *it just remains on the surface,* and so the Evil One comes along and plucks it right out of that person's heart. This is the seed the farmer scatters on the road.

The seed cast in the gravel—this is the person who hears and instantly responds with enthusiasm. *But there is no soil of character, and so when the emotions wear off and some difficulty arrives,* there is nothing to show for it.

The seed cast in the weeds is the person who hears the kingdom news, but *weeds of worry and illusions about getting more and wanting everything under the sun* strangle what was heard, and nothing comes of it.

The seed cast on good earth is *the person who hears and takes in the News, and then produces a harvest beyond his wildest dreams.*"[3]

While these passages are significant from a number of angles, they are displayed here—and particularly those segments which are italicized—to illustrate not only some of the ways in which God gently pursues his creatures, but also to indicate a number of practical barriers that can clog a reciprocal closeness. And all of this, while contributory to producing an external harvest, is initially and progressively *inwardness,* to do with "the heart."

4. Insights about Presence

The sense of presence is a theme permeating both Old and New Testaments. In the book of Exodus, Moses asks Yahweh to teach him his ways, and reminds Yahweh that the nation led by him belongs to Yahweh. Yahweh then replies:

"My Presence will go with you, and I will give you rest."
Then Moses said to him, "If your Presence does not go with us, do not send us up from here. How will anyone know that you are pleased with me and with your people unless you go with us?" (Exodus 33:14–15)

God's undertaking here is both individual, towards Moses, and corporate, towards the fledgling nation. At times the Presence is a fire; at times, a cloud; and at times, a "glory" called *shekinah*. Objectively it is "being with"; subjectively it may be hard to describe, but it moves human beings into states of awe, wonder, love, or expressive emotion. In the Psalms it is

---

3. Petersen, *The Message*, 1769–70. My emphases.

ever-present. In the book of Lamentations, the Daughter of Zion is told: "Pour out your heart like water in the presence of the Lord" (Lam 2:19b).

If we return to the story of Moses, we discover: "The Lord would speak to Moses *face-to-face* as one speaks to a friend" (Exod 33:11, my emphases) And further:

> When Moses came down from Mount Sinai with the two tablets of the covenant law in his hands, he was not aware that *his face was radiant* because he had spoken with the Lord. (Exod 34:29)

Similarly, the Aaronic blessing includes reference to "the face" as follows:

> "The Lord bless you and keep you;
> The Lord *make his face shine on you* and be gracious to you;
> The Lord *turn his face toward you* and give you peace." (Numbers 6:24–26)

The reference to the face seems to indicate an outward expression of the inward heart, and the phrase "face-to-face" strongly suggests a relationship, not of equality, but certainly of intimacy and sharing. As the result of such sharing, there was an inner enrichment which, in Moses' case, was expressed in a way that could not but be recognized by those who observed him. When God is truly present, then, and makes his face shine on a person, the expectation, for that person, is inner and outer radiance leading into *shalom*.

The New Testament took up these themes and found them exemplified and deepened in Jesus. Thus Paul declares:

> God, who said, "Let light shine out of darkness," made his light shine in our hearts to give us the light of the knowledge of God's glory displayed in the face of Christ. (2 Corinthians 4:6)

Christian history includes many, both individuals and communities, who have sought the presence of God through his Son, Jesus Christ. Augustine of Hippo, in the fourth century of the Christian faith, revealed his inner searches with amazing clarity and transparency, as did Francis of Assisi and many others. In the seventeenth century a simple monk, Brother Lawrence, devoted himself, as the title of the book containing his conversations and letters reveals, to *The Practice of the Presence of God*. Such practice required not only silence, but a disciplining of attention within the silence. The list goes on and would certainly include Søren Kierkegaard, the Danish writer of the nineteenth century, who deplored the nominalism of institutionalized religion, with its lack of concern about the individual's search for the presence of God, and the desperate nature of inner experience without God. The fact is that, within biblical history and particularly the Christian era, there has been a strong tradition of meditation and inward exploration. There have been times when this tradition has not characterized the church as a whole, but it has always been there somewhere, and has emerged with force, at particular times, both to energize and to bring peace.

5. Insights about the Paraclete

The Paraclete is one who stands alongside us to defend us, comfort us, or counsel us. The Paraclete is the Holy Spirit whom the Father, at the request of Jesus, has been sent to be with his followers at the present time and right through the future. The Paraclete came to represent Jesus, especially when the "flesh-and-blood" Jesus had to been taken away. He is, by nature, Jesus' *alter-ego*. The world which is hostile to God cannot see him or know him, but the believer knows him because the Spirit lives *within* the believer. Says Alastair Campbell:

> Jesus has drawn the disciples into the same relationship with God that he has modelled for them during his earthly life. We are still living in the light of "that day" and to all of us who love him he promises that Father and Son—God in all his fullness—*will make their home with us*.[4]

This "in-ness" phenomenon is perhaps best illustrated in words within Jesus' prayer for his present and future followers:

> "My prayer is not for them alone. I pray also for those who will believe in me through their message, that all of them may be one, Father, just as *you are in me and I am in you. May they also be in us*." (John 17:20,21)

Paul also emphasizes the same relational inwardness by frequent repetition:

> You, however, are not controlled by the sinful nature but are in the Spirit, if indeed the Spirit of God *lives in you* . . . And if the Spirit of him who raised Jesus from the dead is *living in you*, he who raised Christ from the dead will also give life to your mortal bodies because of his Spirit, who *lives in you*. (Romans 8:9a, 11)

---

4. Campbell, *Encounter with God*, 52.

Walking Alongside

It is important to note, however, that what I have called "relational inwardness" has its significance not solely in moments of intimate awareness, but in something more permanent which begins to characterize the change in the believer's personality. This is put into psychological language by David Dockery,

> J. Murray comments that "the mind of the Spirit is *the dispositional complex,* including the exercise of reason, feeling, and will, patterned after and controlled by the Holy Spirit." The renewing of the mind (Romans 12:2) which was formerly hostile to God (Romans 8:7) can only be achieved by the Spirit."[5]

6. Insights about process

(a) Centered prayer

The chief biblical exemplar of inwardness was Jesus Christ himself. At the beginning of his three years of service there was a concentrated attack upon him by Satan. The scene was a lonely desert place. Jesus' agenda was how to convey his extraordinary concept of the kingdom of God to his own people, and how to accomplish God's destiny for him in life, death, and resurrection. Satan's agenda was to divert Jesus' mind towards personal power and recognition for their own sakes, and to entice Jesus' dependence away from God towards any other conceivable center. Though physically weakened by fasting, Jesus in his replies to Satan's subtle proposals fastened his attention on segments of the Old Testament Scriptures which were relevant and uncompromising, yielding nothing to divergent alternatives. Satan left, at least for a time! Little outward action by Jesus, but huge inward activity!

The three years of service were marked by extraordinary journeys, public teaching, forthright debates with critics, frequent healings, constant mentoring, intimate friendships, and personal conversations. The one thing he could not do without was prayer to the Father in quiet places. One of the most precious pieces of literature throughout all time is his extended prayer for his disciples, present and future, in John 17.

In the hours immediately prior to his trials and crucifixion, he draws aside with his disciples to a quiet garden, and in prayer anticipates the horror of sin-bearing upon the cross. It is instructive that, on this occasion, he

---

5. Dockery, "An Outline of Paul's View of the Spiritual Life," 341–2. My emphases.

craves the empathetic partnership of the disciples. They could have shared his agonizing moments of decision, proving that inwardness could be corporate as well as individual. But they were too sleepy! His struggle finished in resolute love. On the cross itself, his inward communication with the Father occurred, as did his prayer for those executing him.

(b) Focus, intimacy, and prayer

The New Testament writers urged their readers constantly to *focus on Jesus*, as they trod the path of inwardness. For example, Matthew records Jesus' simple invitation:

> Come to me, all you who are weary and burdened, and I will give you rest. Take my yoke upon you and learn from me, for I am gentle and humble in heart, and you will find rest for your souls. (Matthew 11:28–9)

(c) Focus, renewal, and prayer

Paul, while writing with some passion to the recalcitrant Corinthian church, makes several penetrating references, in chapter 4, to aspects of inwardness introduced previously. The first displays the light of God shining in our hearts with the glory in the face of Christ. The second links our inward experiences with the need to focus our attention in the appropriate direction.

> For what we preach is not ourselves, but Jesus Christ as Lord, and ourselves as your servants for Jesus' sake. For God, who said, "Let light shine out of darkness," *made his light shine in our hearts* to give us the light of the knowledge of God's glory displayed *in the face of Christ*. (2 Cor 4:5–6)
>
> Therefore we do not lose heart. Though outwardly we are wasting way, yet *inwardly we are being renewed day by day*. For our light and momentary troubles are achieving for us an eternal glory that far outweighs them all. *So we fix our eyes* not on what is seen, but on what is unseen, since what is seen is temporary, but on what is unseen is eternal. (2 Cor 4:16–18)

Walking Alongside

(d) Flux, permanence, and inner renewal

Implicit in a number of these references is a recognition of the sweep of time, commencing with God's creativity in bringing light out of darkness and order out of chaos in a far-distant past; continuing through the present with a gradual renewing of believers; and finally ensuring consummation at some stage in the future. At this latter time the transformation of believers and their understanding will have been completed: a change from a clouded mirror-like reflection, to a full face-to-face knowledge of God and of themselves. Christian inwardness, then, acknowledges and works within the realities of past, present, and future. In the words of the writer to the Hebrews: "Jesus Christ is the same yesterday and today and for ever" (13:8)

Robert C. Roberts makes this point well. He starts by quoting an extract from Isaiah 40 which commences, "All people are like grass" and finishes with the reflection, "The grass withers and the flowers fall." The final balancing comment, however, is: "but the word of our God endures forever." Roberts continues by claiming that those who view their own lives with honesty "will welcome the thought that there is *an enduring rock amidst the flux of things* . . . In the Christian perspective Isaiah is preaching the really good news that God's loving disposition toward us—his word of mercy and comfort—endures forever and cannot be turned aside."[6]

To affirm seriously that everything is in flux—that *everything* is changing constantly—presents us either with a God who himself is changing as his relationships with his creatures alter, which is the stance of the Process Theologians; or otherwise with a world that has no enduring standards by which to make judgments of morality, or sanity, or appropriate attitudes. When "anything goes" it's fun for a while, but hell in the longer term! When this has been said, however, there is no denying the flux of things in the contemporary world, nor the fact that things become more complex, and do so with greater acceleration than the world has ever known. To make this observation is not a subtle way to invite conservatism in social and political matters. The withering grass and the enduring rock have often, in partnership, prompted radical programs of reform.

---

6. Roberts, *Spirituality and Human Emotion*, 28–9.

C. MINDFULNESS IN CURRENT COUNSELING

1. Buddhist meditation and therapy

It would not be an exaggeration to say that in the last decade the approach which has dominated counseling in the Western world is what has been called "mindfulness." We shall shortly look at some definitions of mindfulness, but even prior to doing this, it would be justifiable to call it a form of inwardness. It has been derived, in general, from a Buddhist approach to insight meditation called Vipassana, and many helpful outcomes have been described from its use, varying from peace of mind for anyone, to release from chronic depression and addictions for some.

The advocates of mindfulness, however, are not on the whole content that it should be regarded as merely another therapy. Belinda Siew Luan Zhong, for example, who is an academic in a secular Australian university, makes this point in an article entitled "Expanding the Understanding of Mindfulness: Seeing the Tree and the Forest":

> Currently, meditation and mindfulness practices are probably the more familiar and accepted expressions of the *dhamma* [the Buddhist understanding and experience of life]. However, the popularity of these practices has sometimes led practitioners to overlook other aspects of the Buddha's teachings. As a result, mindfulness is often leveled down to a technique, rather than an attitude towards living... My meditation teacher... said to me "It is not how long you sit in meditation. Your whole life is meditation." I learned then that it is through acquiring a meditative attitude that one gains peace of mind.[7]

In similar vein, Mark A. Lau declares:

> Mindfulness... has a quality of fullness and impeccability to it, a bringing of our *whole heart and mind,* our full attention, to each moment.[8]

There are grounds for wondering, then, whether mindfulness is an approach to therapy in itself, or whether, to be effective, it is actually the first step into a way of life which is philosophically distinctive, making claims as extensive as those of Christianity. Whether that way of life constitutes a religion is a really difficult issue to decide. The "Lesser Vehicle" of Buddhism,

---

7. Zhong, "Expanding the Understanding of Mindfulness," 120,122.
8. Lau, *Mindfulness-Based Cognitive Therapy Workshop Tour 2009,* 9.

termed Hinayana, which claims to pass on the orthodox teachings of the Buddha, recognizes no gods and hence could only be styled a comprehensive philosophy of life. The "Greater Vehicle," termed Mahayana, of which Tibetan Buddhism is a variant, does acknowledge deities. Whatever the situation about deities, however, focusing our whole heart and mind on anything would be recognized, within the biblical faith, as *worship*, the only appropriate object for which would be God himself. Perhaps a meditative attitude would remind a Christian of a prayerful attitude. Once again, however, humanistic meditation is concerned usually with self-discovery and self-conversation; while prayer involves conversation with God, even though there would also be a reverberation into self-understanding.

2. Definitions of mindfulness

Because mindfulness is an experiential term, we can expect some divergence in the way it is defined, or better, described by various authors and practitioners. Zhong, for example, says:

> Mindfulness helps us to be aware of awareness—being aware of what we are feeling, thinking, experiencing, or doing when we are doing it, and to interrupt the circuit before the rumination starts. ["Rumination" refers to the stream of consciousness or the clutter of thoughts in the mind, mentioned in Part A above.] . . . We become "a disinterested spectator of phenomena."[9]

Lau's description includes one element not mentioned by Zhong, but recognized by most others in the field. He says:

> Mindfulness means *paying attention* in a particular way; on purpose, in the present moment and non-judgmentally . . . [It] means seeing how things are, directly and immediately, seeing for oneself that which is present and true.[10]

The authors of *The Mindful Way through Depression* comment that "our individual lines of research ultimately led us to examine the clinical use of meditative practices oriented toward cultivating a particular form of awareness, known as mindfulness."[11] They add, "Mindfulness could also be described as 'heartfulness' because it is really about a compassionate

---

9. Zhong, "Expanding the Understanding of Mindfulness," 130, 131. My Emphases.
10. Lau, *Mindfulness-Based Cognitive Therapy Workshop Tour 2009*, 9.
11. Williams, M. et al., *The Mindful Way through Depression*, 5.

Inwardness

awareness" [Note the apparent contradiction between this emphasis and Zhong's "disinterested spectator" stance] and further, " . . . there is an unsuspected power in inhabiting the moment you're living in right now with full awareness."[12]

These authors also make the point, which is found routinely in discussions of mindfulness, that it is "a way of shifting from *doing* to *being*."[13]

D. DANIEL SIEGEL AND THE MINDFUL BRAIN[14]

1. A twofold approach

In chapter 6, "Relationships," we mentioned with appreciation an earlier book by Siegel and Hartzell, entitled *Parenting from the Inside Out*. This emphasized the significance of attachment studies to the nurture of children, and also drew attention to the fact that the brain can be changed by experience, and is a highly social organ. In the Preface to *The Mindful Brain*, Siegel describes the process whereby he was inspired to review existing research "in the field of mindfulness-based clinical interventions."[15] His interest was directed now to encompassing the links, first of all, between relationships and brain functioning, in which his expertise and natural teaching ability were already established; and then between these and mind. In his own words:

> I love science and am thrilled to learn from empirical explorations into the deep nature of ourselves and our world. But I am also a clinician, steeped in the world of subjective experience. Our internal world is real, though it may not be quantifiable in ways that science often requires for careful analysis. In the end, our subjective lives are not reducible to our neural functioning.[16]

At this point, because of the complexity and comprehensive coverage of *The Mindful Brain*, what follows will take the form of an extensive critical review of what undoubtedly will become a highly influential volume on the nature and therapeutic possibilities of mindfulness.

---

12. Ibid., 5 and 7.
13. Ibid., 54.
14. Siegel, *The Mindful Brain*.
15. Ibid., xix.
16. Ibid., xviii.

2. The formative subjective discoveries

In chapters three and four, Siegel describes his experience, shared with 100 scientists, most of whom had an interest in the brain, of *a week of silence*. It was at first very difficult, but as the days went on, he recorded significant changes. One such follows:

> There's a strange change today. It feels as if some part of my mind that was aching to connect with others has given up aiming for them and has turned inward toward myself. I feel a surge of awareness of each step, a kind of connection to myself that wasn't there before ... Each step is unique. There's no place other than here, no moment other than now. I'm filled with excitement. I feel a floating sensation ... each moment inflated with a kind of helium from my mind. I want to tell someone, so I tell myself.[17]

The thing that I find exciting here is an author who gives attention equally to neuroscience, on the one hand, and inner experience on the other; and then attempts to create meaningful links between them, for the sake of living in general and therapeutic interventions in particular. I'm not sure whether this has been attempted before, or, if it has, with such artistry. In addition to all of this, there is a modesty and tentativeness apparent in Siegel's hypotheses. Along with this admiration, however, I am aware of being somewhat uneasy about "the turn inward toward myself." In chapter one of Siegel's remarkable book, he sets out, in summary form, the themes that will be elaborated in later chapters. The following two sentences deal with one such, and may help to make my present point:

> With mindfulness seen as a form of intrapersonal attunement, it may be possible to reveal the mechanisms by which *we become our own best friend* with mindful practice. We would treat our best friend with kindness, after all.[18]

My uneasiness is due, not to the possibility of self-understanding in itself, nor to being well disposed to looking after oneself, but rather to what is central in all of these interlinked processes. Siegel, and those generally who propose a mindfulness track, start with some inborn ability to make truthful appraisals and to show genuine compassion to themselves, and then are enabled to express these to their fellow humans; and thus because they adopt a basically humanist viewpoint, God finds no place in the process.

17. Ibid., 61.
18. Ibid., 16. My emphases.

Inwardness

The biblical approach denies the possibility of generating one's own unsullied capabilities, and therefore relies upon a loving and searching God, to display his good news and, where there is genuine response, to begin his work of character transformation individually and corporately. Relationship with God, for the Christian, is primary, and leads towards relationship with others and also with ourselves.

3. Mind and mindfulness

Siegel gives a clear and brief idea, firstly, of what he means by *the mind*. It is "a process that regulates the flow of energy and information."[19] There have been many ways of defining the mind, both by philosophers and psychologists over the centuries, but this definition, with its physiological and neurological slant, seems relatively new. It is different, at least on the surface, from the emphases of biblical writers spelled out earlier in this book. It does, however, make a distinction between mind and brain, and therefore runs counter to the brain-mind identity theorists of the mid-twentieth century. The definition serves the purpose of being sufficiently clear for important connections to be made in this era of neuroscience.

Next, Siegel deals with the idea of *mindfulness*:

> With mindful awareness the flow of energy and information that is our mind enters our conscious attention and we can both appreciate its contents and also come to regulate its flow in a new way. Mindful awareness... actually involves more than just simply being aware: It involves being aware of aspects of the mind itself. Instead of being on automatic and mindless, mindfulness helps us awaken, and by reflecting on the mind we are enabled to make choices and thus change becomes possible.[20]

It will be seen from this quotation that mindfulness is described partly in terms of what it is, but then partly in terms of *what it is not*. He tells the story of Diane Ackerman, a naturalist, who suffered a bad accident in Japan, whereby a number of her ribs were broken, and it was a struggle to breathe. Ackerman approached her ordeal

> with curiosity, openness, acceptance, and love [abbreviated by Siegel as the acronym COAL]. This mindset enabled her to learn

19. Ibid., 5.
20. Ibid., 5,6.

> from the event, to gather the internal strength she needed to hold on, literally, and to not only survive in spite of the accident, but to thrive because of it. This distinction between awareness with COAL and just paying attention with *preconceived ideas that imprison the mind,* ("I shouldn't have hit my foot, I'm so clumsy. Why did I fall off this cliff? What is wrong with me!") is the difference that makes all the difference. This is the difference between being aware, and being mindfully aware.[21]

4. The prison-house

To begin with, we must go back to the story of the heroic Diane Ackerman. We are not told whether this woman had previously developed an attitude of "mindfulness" in the terms described by Siegel. What is clear, however, is that she displayed mature responses in a very challenging situation, as many other human beings have done over the centuries. Certainly some outstanding examples of such action are given in the Christian Scriptures, with Jesus Christ and the apostle Paul heading the list. And it would be fair to say that, in their case, motivation and action were drawn from a distinctive set of issues, including their understanding of the past, and the beckoning nature of a future kingdom.

Chiefly, however, we draw attention in the above quotation to the notion of "imprisonment." In many places within the book, Siegel refers to what he considers the detrimental effect of "top-down" influences such as

> preconceptions of shoulds and ought-to's [which] are choking us from living mindfully, of being kind to ourselves. The term *top-down* refers to the way our memories, beliefs, and emotions shape our "bottom-up" direct sensations of experience. Kindness to ourselves is what gives us the strength and resolve to break out of that top-down prison and approach life's events, planned or unplanned, with curiosity, openness, acceptance, and love."[22]

Now the "shoulds" and "ought to's" mentioned above might be generously interpreted by the reader as petty self-instructions of an overcautious kind. But, in fact, they are far more inclusive. Siegel, again:

---

21. Ibid., 16.
22. Ibid., 16.

Inwardness

> With the process of mindfulness, we can awaken from *automaticity* to not be "enslaved" by the large-scale dynamics set up by earlier experience and embedded in beliefs in the form of mental *models of right and wrong and judgments of good and bad.*[23]

So while top-down experiences include the mental clutter and chatter, i.e., the constant thought-stream, referred to earlier, which certainly can prove invasive if not controlled; they also include, for Siegel, the moral categories of right and wrong, good and bad. Perhaps it is thinking of this kind that has influenced counselors to shun the use of "shoulds" under all circumstances, in recent times. Morality, however, can never be restricted to the findings of individuals who have become deeply self-aware. It is honed out of basic beliefs and the cumulative findings, throughout history, of whole societies and wise observers. It cannot be commenced from scratch individually, however aware and informed any individual might be. It must, of course, be *owned* by the individual concerned. Apart from the question of morality, is it valid to reduce those who are not aware of their own awareness—technically, lacking "meta-awareness"—to the level of being mindless and being automata? *Is* their state of limited awareness a prison? Or do we look for imprisonment, of both the aware and the meta-aware, elsewhere?

5. Then, now, ever

Included in the villainy of the top-down influences are the notions of past, present, and future. Siegel maintains:

> Things as they are clash with things as our top-down invariant processes expect them to be. We shove sensation through the filter of the past to make the future predictable. In the process, we lose the present. But because *the present is all that exists*, we have lost everything in the bargain. It seems as simple as this. But it isn't so easy to undo because top-down influences that enslave bottom-up living have potent neural connectivity backing them up—much more powerful than the uncertainty of living in the here-and-now. And for this reason being mindful requires intention, and courage.[24]

---

23. Ibid., 135.
24. Ibid., 151. My emphases.

Walking Alongside

It is genuinely confusing to know what Siegel is concerned about here. Psychologically, all experienced counselors will recognize the conscious, or unconscious, influences that the past—especially past relationships—can have on the present behavior patterns of clients; seen, perhaps in the most extreme form, in those who are addicted to something which is recognizable, but also in those afflicted with obsessive or compulsive tendencies, which may lack identifiable origins. But are there not many instances also, of those who have suffered great difficulties in past experience, but have made their adjustments in such a way that they may now recognize and even describe the past, without allowing it to dominate the present? We tend to call them "well adjusted." In these cases, how do the levels of the brain, as described by Siegel, dominate the present? Freedom from such domination—even from the pressure of the Freudian "superego"—is fairly regularly achieved through approaches which are distinct from meditation. The outlines of *the prison* can become rather dim!

When it is claimed, then, that *the present is all that exists*, it sounds like an assertion of metaphysical faith. Yes, there is always uncertainty involved in living in the here-and-now; and yes, it requires intention and courage; but there seems no good reason to eliminate the lessons of the past, or to exclude a credible view of the future, especially when, as in Christianity, the one Figure and Point-of-Reference straddles past, present, and future, and claims to provide transformation even in times of suffering.

6. Awareness, intention, and attunement

Siegel emphasizes later in his book, "an awareness of awareness itself and a focus of *attention on intention*."[25] With respect to the latter: "Intentions create an integrated stage of priming, a gearing up of our neural system to be in the mode of that specific intention: we can be readying to receive, to sense, to focus, to behave in a certain manner."[26] It is in this way that he makes a significant link between the inwardness that is chiefly his concern, and the outwardness of action. However, over and above this link, is what Siegel terms an intrapersonal *attunement*.

There is a further significant link hypothesized. By harnessing the "social circuits of mirroring"—that is the activation of mirror neurons—and empathy, he maintains that we can come to "feel felt" by another person

25. Ibid., 176. My emphases.
26. Ibid., 177.

while the other person can "feel felt" by us; and thus there is some kind of neurological basis for the formation of a personal relationship. This is described as involving *inter*personal mechanisms. It is also claimed that when two people become attuned to each other in this way, a desirable state of "neural integration" is created within each. The "significant link," referred to above, comes about as follows:

> If we apply this analysis [i.e., of the mechanisms involved in the *inter*personal dynamic] to the notion that the self-other shifting in mindfulness is actually between *self-as-observing* and *self-as-experiencing*, then we have a neural formula for self-empathy, or internal attunement. Here the social circuits of the brain are focused on experiencing self as an "other" that can be understood, received without judgment, and attuned to . . . by the observing self.[27]

Thus the formula for the *inter*personal mechanisms is applied to *intra*personal dynamics along with a listing of profound emergent benefits, including a state of neural integration, and a way of engaging the self with curiosity, acceptance, and love (without fear). Herein, of course, we see the strength of Siegel's approach to relationships, noted and appreciated earlier, and employing the fairly recent mechanism of mirror neurons.

From the viewpoint of Christian theology, we need a third category, emphasizing the presence of the Holy Spirit—within the dynamic between self-as-observer and self-as-experiencer—who reveals Christ and fashions for us a relationship with him. Perhaps because the Spirit has been called "Paraclete" (in Greek: "called alongside"), we might introduce *para*personal dynamics to penetrate the two kinds already recognized.

7. The core self

It is interesting to find Siegel, who has been inspired by and has largely adopted Vipassana meditation, a traditional Buddhist approach, speaking about the ideal of developing a "core self." A widespread understanding of Buddhist doctrine is that any identifiable self should gradually be reduced to the point where individuality and identity would be attenuated, and what remained would be integrated into "the whole" as a drop of water into the wide ocean. From more recent investigation, however, it becomes clear that

27. Ibid., 132. My emphases.

just as Christianity continues with many internal divisions, so Buddhism presents with many different faces. In view of the above, then, it is true that in wanting to see the development of a deep and rich "core self" Siegel, on this precise point, sides with Christian anthropology, rather than what has been traditionally understood as the Buddhist approach. Let us interact with his view now, in some detail, and in his own words. We commence with his testimony about "the silent week," and what followed from it:

> And so, for me, awareness of sensation, observation, and concept enabled automaticity to be decoupled. But during the week of silent retreat it became clear that these three streams did more than give me that freedom in the moment, it opened a subterranean stream of awareness, that spring of non-conceptual knowing, that somehow held it altogether. In silence at first I felt I could lose my mind, as all of my usual external anchors were gone and the ship of my psyche lost its moorings. But as time went on it seemed that I came instead to find my mind . . . Attuning inwardly felt like a welcome home celebration.[28]

This was clearly a conversion, and, if it was not clear before, it must now become clear that conversions happen in many circumstances, and such changes are related to many different focal points. Siegel's experience emerged as he became aware of his awareness. He now goes on to describe "personal identity," or "I," but in a way that distinguishes it from the basic or core self, to which he gives the new name: *the ipseitious self* or *the bare self*.

> Our personal identity is filled with adaptations to a lifelong list of experiences from our earliest days forward. In many ways, the layers of memory that embed these events and our ways of coping with them form at the scaffold of neural connectivity within the brain that serves to organize our lives. This organizational structure we call "I" is filled with the top-down influences we have been exploring. These invariant representations have been reinforced by emotional arousal which enhances neuroplasticity. They have also been a part of a re-entry loop in which we carry out behaviors based on a certain identity, and the world responds in a particular way to us. We then respond back to how others treat us, and that in turn engrains our patterns of processing and solidifies our personal identity even further . . . We can see then that both synaptic connections (memory) and interpersonal responses (social interactive habits), converge upon a personal

28. Ibid., 149.

identity that we then carry around with us as a transparent cloak that constrains how we live our lives. Mindful awareness is an opportunity to make the cloak of personal identity visible, to see beneath its surface textures.[29]

Presumably every human being, at any rate in our contemporary world, develops an "I" which, because of neuronal circuitry, memories, and social expectations, is constrained with respect to the way it lives; or to use Siegel's more usual images, is imprisoned, or progressing on automatic, somewhat like a zombie! This is a state of affairs from which, apparently, we all need to be rescued. The "core" or "bare" self is able to be deeply aware of the person's own awarenesses, either when stripped of the offending cloak, or in a position, by seeing through it, to bring transformation through mindfulness. It now "sees" the personal identity, but, as it were, stands alongside it with a monitoring, and finally a transforming role.

8. A broad theory

This, then, is virtually a complete view of human nature which diagnoses its flaws, and indicates the kind of salvation that is appropriate. In principle there is nothing wrong with spelling out such a structure. Plausibility, however, has to be considered. One wonders how it is that some children, who have had a life enriched by attachment, are to be placed in a similar developmental pattern with those who have been totally deprived. And finally, if an "I" or personal identity appears, which displays openness and self-awareness through processes of growth which do not include mindfulness, would there be an appropriate neurological story to accompany or explain this situation?

In certain ways, Siegel is saying, with the apostle Paul: "Do not conform to the pattern of this world . . . "—"the world," in this case, being all top-down influences, including those reinforced by social conformity and societal patterns—" . . . but be transformed by the renewing of your mind,"[30] the renewing process, in this case, being the practice of mindfulness. But whereas Siegel sees transformation as an interaction between brain functioning and certain disciplined forms of attention to intention,

---

29. Ibid., 149–150.
30. Romans 12:2.

and awareness of awareness, which are at least available to human beings out of their own resources, Paul sees such transformation differently.

Paul's exhortation to his readers is that, with God's past and present mercy to them in mind, they should offer their very selves to him—a reasonable act—and let him do the transforming and the renewing, though with their goodwill and participation.

E. INWARDNESS: REVIEW AND SUMMARY

1. A current approach to counseling

Mindfulness, at the beginning of the twenty-first century, has figured prominently among practical approaches to counseling. It has drawn significantly upon Buddhist practices of meditation, honed over several thousands of years. It features attention procedures which require a deliberate focus within the present moment, and are carried through with a non-judgmental approach. These purport to produce a degree of control over disturbing thoughts and emotions through the awareness of bodily sensations, commencing with the breathing process. Many clients appear to have been helped by these means.

Most counselors, including Christians, would not wish to rule out approaches which give relief from existing psychological pain for distressed clients, merely on the basis that such approaches had arisen from a belief-system which is clearly not their own. Multiple approaches to counseling have appeared in the course of the twentieth century, whatever their ideological background, and have been recognized in the counseling profession as helpful, even if not healing. Many have been seen as virtually neutral, philosophically and religiously. And so just as many ways have been discovered by surgeons to penetrate the body, many ways, over the centuries, have been found by therapists to gain entry to the human psyche. Meditation would be seen as one of these.

2. An exciting attempt at convergence between science and mindfulness

Precisely because Daniel Siegel has made a systematic move to integrate experience and science in the interests of therapy, we have examined in some detail his assertions about the effects of mindfulness on people and their relationships. His comprehensive theorizing, as mentioned earlier, includes a particular interpretation of everyday living, in which the interaction between normal brain functioning and the social environment yields a lifestyle which he frequently refers to as "imprisonment," and in which the individual comes to live an inflexible "automatic" existence. Such a lifestyle is brought about through "top-down" influences, including "mental models of right and wrong and judgments of good and bad" which are moral categories. And finally he develops the idea of "a core self." Becoming aware of sensation, observation, and concept through mindful attention opened up for Siegel, "a subterranean stream of awareness, that spring of non-conceptual knowing, that somehow held it all together."[31] The true "I" is what is aware of all other awarenesses and intentions, and thus has the power to control and determine them. This theory, then, has its own doctrine of flawed human nature, and its own doctrine of salvation, emerging with its own version of personal and interpersonal fruitfulness. It is a new gospel where all the ingredients are humanly derived. It is a great deal more than an alternative slant on therapy.

In spite of helpful linkages acknowledged earlier in this chapter, our view is that Siegel has erected one model, linking experience with neuroscience, but that other models could be constructed out of the same scientific materials with comparable plausibility. It is not the case that we are challenging his knowledge in the area of neuroscience; to do that would be simply naive. What the Christian church needs at the moment is someone as competent as Siegel in neuroscience, and with an ability as passionate as Siegel's, to see connections between neuroscience and the Christian view of inwardness.

There are probably several Christian scholars who bid fair to fill this need. One of these would certainly be Joel B. Green, Professor of New Testament Interpretation, at Fuller Theological Seminary in California. His book, *Body, Soul, and Human Life*, brings together evidence from Scripture and from neuroscience on what we have called "inwardness." Kevin Corcoran of Calvin College, one of the scholars affirming Green's work on the back cover of his book, claims:

> Far from telling different and irreconcilable stories about human nature, Joel Green helps us to see that these two sources—the Bible and the neurosciences—actually tell mutually enriching and

---

31. Siegel, *The Mindful Brain*, 149.

> complementary stories about what it means to be fully human and fully alive.

While Green refers, with appreciation, to the work of Siegel, he does not give his attention to the issues which I have raised above. His expertise and his total emphasis would, however, allow him to do so. In the meantime, then, our analysis of Siegel's book and our presentation of a biblical approach to inwardness remain.

3. The Christian presupposition

The concern of this book has been to bring to the surface theological truths that could underlie the thought and practice of Christians who undertake to counsel fellow human beings. One such truth is that God searches the hearts of people with a view to their responding positively to his love-initiative in Christ. When the heart is searched and the life orientation is challenged, a dynamic commences which involves inner experience. Its outcome, of course, varies from person to person.

The Scriptures say a great deal about inwardness, and the attempt has been made, in section A, to cover a number of the emphases given, as well as indicating briefly the rich historical tradition of inwardness in the Christian era. The heart, or "core self," of the person cries out for a focus, and when such is found, reflects it, certainly in outward action and shared relationship, but also inwardly. In the hustle and bustle of life—and in the battles with sin, sometimes won, but all too frequently lost—there is the need to concentrate attention on Christ, as well as drawing aside to listen, in the silence, to his Spirit who now has made a home within. Jesus, with his reliance on prayer, in good times and bad, remains the model. There are, of course, factors that interfere with the growth of inner union, needing both recognition and treatment. As Christian life progresses, however, there normally grows a relationship between Christ and the believer which yields hints, at least, of Presence and face-to-face knowing: an ever-increasing glory. And though rapid change characterizes the beginning of the twenty-first century, Jesus ensures a hidden permanence through his own changeless character.

For some clients, these matters will be completely foreign. For others they will be part-and-parcel of what can be brought to the counseling room to note and to discuss. For the Christian counselor they can feature as an understanding, a mark of personal living, and, in part, a lens through which to interpret a human problem, and beyond that, a human life.

Having dealt, now, with human beings, with God's character as he engages them, and with some goals of life and of counseling, we conclude by discussing a question of practicability. What is the feasibility of practicing Christian presuppositions within counseling, bearing in mind the secular requirements of a liberal democracy? This is the problem faced in the final chapter.

10

Profession

The title of this chapter is a play on words—a "pun"! It attempts to spell out three aspects of *Christian profession*, that is, three ways in which we profess or exhibit the Christian faith. It turns attention, simultaneously, to the acceptability within the *counseling profession* of those three ways.

A. WITNESS

1. Wordless speech

With respect to Christian profession, the point of departure for the first of the three ways would be Jesus' words from the Sermon on the Mount:

> You [disciples] are the light of the world. A city on a hill cannot be hidden. Neither do people light a lamp and put it under a bowl. Instead they put it on its stand, and it gives light to everyone in the house. In the same way, *let your light shine before others, that they may see your good deeds and glorify your Father in heaven.* (Matthew 5:14–16)

We shall give the name "*witness*" to this way of declaring the faith, while recognizing that the word sometimes refers to *all* aspects of Christian profession. Witness, then, covers that aspect of inner life that so permeates the speech and behavior of a Christian that it may well be noted by an interested observer. The more constant it is, even while allowing for variations of expression, the more recognizable it is; the more transparent, the less "under-a-bowl," the less it is problematic in the mind of the watcher. Granted that the Christian in question will be tempted and sinful in some situations, the remorse and repentance which follow may, in themselves, become a sign of genuineness. One fascinating example of witness is the advice, given by Peter in his first letter, to husbands and wives, but particularly that given to wives who are married to unbelieving husbands:

> Your beauty should not come from outward adornment, such as elaborate hairstyles and the wearing of gold jewelry and fine clothes. Rather, it should be that of your inner self, the unfading beauty of a gentle and quiet spirit, which is of great worth in God's sight. (1 Peter 3:3–4)

Let us grant that "outward adornment" will vary from culture to culture, and century to century! The main point, however, is perfectly clear. First, it would seem to be implied that the closer the relationship between believer and unbeliever, the more readily the inner self, while greatly valued by God, will be recognized and valued also by the observer; in this case, the spouse. Also the unfading beauty, the purity, and reverence of a person in touch with the Spirit (see Romans 8:16), is able to be perceived by the non-Christian, and to constitute a winsome message.

2. Wordless counseling

In the counseling situation, we have noted already that the relationship developing between counselor and client is an important factor, and frequently a therapeutic one, in the total dynamic. It is almost inevitable, therefore, that the quality of the counselor's inner life will be conveyed to the client over a number of sessions. This may be due partly to the curiosity of the client, but will often function as a comparison between the present counseling relationship, on the one hand, and, on the other, those "real life" relationships from the past which have been unrewarding, disappointing, or even destructive. Of course this situation may be clouded, and therefore compromised, by transference or countertransference, but instead it can be exemplary even though imperfect in some respects. Generally the witness of the Christian counselor will at least be recognized by the non-Christian client, and frequently valued, even though the counselor *has not used words* to bring about such response.

Walking Alongside

The challenge to the Christian counselor is not to be intensively introspective or hypercritical of his or her performances in the counseling room. Instead, it is for the counselor to be firmly "attached," as an integral branch, to the "true vine." As Jesus said:

> Remain in me, as I also remain in you. No branch can bear fruit by itself; it must remain in the vine. Neither can you bear fruit unless you remain in me. I am the vine; you are the branches. If you remain in me and I in you, you will bear much fruit; apart from me you can do nothing. (John 15:4,5)

How acceptable, now, is such witness in the counseling profession? Surely there can be nothing unacceptable about it! *Counselors are who they are*, even though always in a process of becoming, whether they are Christian or non-Christian. Who they are will make a significant contribution to their relationship with any one client and, via that relationship, to the quality of that client's life. If this situation were unacceptable for reasons of faith, the only recourse would be to remove all Christians from the profession. This point will be underlined by a story from the life of one of my dearest friends.

David left Australia in 1949 to become a missionary in Western China. Shortly after his arrival, the Communist regime had become supreme, and the implication was that all Christian missionaries must be sent home. At the same time, however, there was an urgent need to enrich the local university with experts in mathematics and physics. David, following an impeccable record in these fields from the University of Sydney, including some innovative research, was such an expert. Having gained a good grasp of Mandarin, he was approached by the Foreign Affairs Bureau to see whether he would be willing to consider helping the university. He then offered to do this saying that he understood the necessary limitation against proselytizing. He knew, of course, that his life would still convey a Christian witness. But the Communists knew it also! In spite of their considerable academic need, his offer was refused. All Christians—along with devotees of other religions—had to be removed or silenced. The ideological stance was rigorous. Fortunately, in many countries today, Christians are tolerated or even welcomed into the counseling profession either in spite of or because of their distinctive contribution.

B. TESTIMONY

1. Answering a question

In chapter 6, dealing with relationships, one of the points made was that "there are occasions, in the lives of certain people, when . . . a relationship, involving an element of self-disclosure [by the counselor] will not only be rewarding and formative for them, but may well, in addition, have therapeutic outcomes." In the story quoted at that point, however, "self-disclosure" seemed to involve the counselor revealing problems in their own past life, which were similar to those being experienced currently by the client, thus producing a sense of identification and mutual understanding.

While the efficacy, in certain cases, of such self-disclosure is clearly important, it is not the only way in which the *reciprocation,* which I claimed earlier was a necessary element in any relationship, could function. In the ebb and flow of counseling conversation, it is by no means rare for matters of religious faith to be included. Sometimes the client will refer to the presence or absence of religion in the process of growing up. This may be either critical or appreciative. Sometimes the issue will involve treatment of the client by a local church body, and have little or nothing to do with a faith experience. In either case, partly because the client needs to bounce these issues off another person, or sometimes because he or she has already heard of the counselor's involvement in a church, a question will be asked about *the counselor's position.*

The first alternative in this situation is that the counselor refuses to reveal a commitment because it might conflict with what is understood to be the counselor's role; or out of fear that to do this might lead on to an uncomfortable disagreement; or that it might entail a huge digression from the main therapeutic goal in mind. The second alternative is merely to answer the client's questions in a realistic, discriminating, and truthful way. This now brings the counselor's profession of faith to a point *where words are or may be used.* There should be no suggestion that the counselor is demanding agreement or has a monopoly on the truth, but only responding in an honest way to a genuine request. This is what, for purposes of the current discussion, I am calling *testimony,* though I am aware that the word can be used, both in Scripture and elsewhere, in different senses. Here it is used in a somewhat similar way to that used in a court of law. It is simple and factual, even though beliefs and feelings lie significantly behind it, *and it is given in response to a question.* The question itself may emerge from curiosity, from a hope that the counselor will affirm the client's position, or from a hostile stance.

2. New Testament questions and answers

Scripture contains clear instances of such testimony. One involves John the Baptist and his sense of identity.

> Now this was John's testimony when the Jewish leaders in Jerusalem sent priests and Levites to ask him who he was. He did not fail to confess, but confessed freely, "I am not the Messiah."
> They asked him, "Then who are you? Are you Elijah?"
> He said, "I am not."
> "Are you the Prophet?" He answered, "No."
> Finally they said, "Who are you? . . . What do you say about yourself?"
> John replied in the words of Isaiah the prophet, "I am the voice of one calling in the wilderness, 'Make straight the way for the Lord.'"
> (John 1:19–23)

Here is a case where the questions came thick and fast, and were answered promptly and accurately. Finally when the interrogators allowed themselves an open question, they received an answer from the Old Testament which was meaningful to them. The passage above describes John's answers as his "testimony."

Another interesting case of testimony, in the way I am using it, is the story of Jesus' healing of the man born blind.[1] This time it is the Pharisees specifically who conduct the questioning. Once again it is a question of identity. Neighbors and others inquired whether the man in question was the same one who used to sit and beg. Some said "Yes," others "No." But the man himself insisted he was the one! Then came the demand:

> "How then were your eyes opened?"
> He replied, "The man they call Jesus made some mud and put it on my eyes. He told me to go to Siloam and wash. So I went and washed, and then I could see." (John 9:10–11)

Later, in a second bout of questioning, when the Pharisees assured the man that Jesus was a sinner, he replied:

---

1. John 9:1–34.

> "Whether he is a sinner or not, I don't know. One thing I do know. I was blind but now I see!" (John 9:25)

This time, under heavy and hostile questioning, the man states simply what he does know and what he does not know. This is simple verbal testimony.

The final example concerns the questioning of Jesus by Pontius Pilate, and once again the issue is one of identity. Pilate asked Jesus directly: "Are you the king of the Jews?" After some further discussion, Jesus said:

> "My kingdom is not of this world. If it were, my servants would fight to prevent my arrest by the Jewish leaders. But now my kingdom is from another place."
> "You are a king, then!" said Pilate.
> Jesus answered, "You say that I am a king. In fact, the reason I was born and came into the world is to testify to the truth. Everyone on the side of truth listens to me." (John 18:33b–37)

This case is similar to the other two in the sense that it is verbal and given in response to questions, but it is different in that it conveys aspects of a new world view and a different interpretation of the word "king," linking it strongly to "truth." Overall it is explanatory, rather than factual. Strangely, Pilate appears to understand at least that Jesus' reply was of an interpretive kind. In these pivotal moments, under crucial questioning, Jesus is giving testimony to the truth. The issue now is whether the Christian counselor is free, when questioned in the process of counseling, to state and if necessary explain his or her faith-commitment.

Finally we should note Peter's advice given to the people of God:

> . . . in your hearts revere Christ as Lord. Always be prepared to give an answer to everyone who asks you to give the reason for the hope that you have. But do this with gentleness and respect, keeping a clear conscience. (1 Peter 3:15–16a)

Recently a client, with whom I had had previous contact, came again to talk about two current issues in his life. One was the disappearance of a much loved pet, presumably dying as the result of a car accident. The other was the discovery of a very compatible woman, following a long series of romantic disappointments in his experience. As a lapsed Catholic, he had returned to desperate praying about the pet, the intensity of which had become something of a problem for his partner who was a professed atheist. He was now being torn between the remnants of his Catholicism, on the one hand, and the plausibility of his partner's atheism, on the other. And yet Christmas had recently come and with it a flood of stories about Jesus which had retained some of their former personal impact for him. There were grief, companionly fulfillment, and a conflict of faith, all struggling within the same personality at the same time. But what he wanted to know most of all from me was how I would discern the faith issue!

Was I, as a Christian, to disown any interest in his dilemma, or, while not able to offer any easy solution, *to interact with him* having my own theological insights as a background factor? I chose the latter course and, in the process, *was giving testimony* to my own belief. Ironically, prior to our next session, the pet had been discovered, wounded and disheveled, and was now in process of being gently restored by my client to full health! At least it was plausible that his prayers had been answered!

As in the case of *witness*, we must now ask what would the attitude of the counseling profession be in cases like the one above, which I have included under the term *testimony*?

4. The codes and counseling-power

It is at this point that we need to refer to several current professional codes of ethics. The first is *Ethical Principles of Psychologists and Code of Conduct*, issued by the American Psychological Association, 2010—hereinafter, "the American Code."[2] The second is the *Code of Ethics*, of the Australian Psychological Society, updated in September 2007, coordinated with *Ethical Guidelines*, whose purpose is "to clarify and amplify the application of the principles established in the *Code* and to facilitate their interpretation in contemporary areas of professional practice."[3] Hereinafter the *Code* and the associated *Guidelines* are referred to as "the Australian Code." Both Codes have been carefully and sensitively prepared and worded, and are based on broad ethical principles, which would be applauded by Christian ethicists; but which have also had to take account of instances of malpractice that have failed to consider the best interests of clients.

The Codes declare that psychologists *recognize the power or authority they hold* over people when practicing as psychologists, and urge that they must always act in the client's best interests. Thus the declaration in the American Code, "3.08 Exploitative Relationships: Psychologists do not

---

2. Adopted August 21, 2002; Effective June 1, 2003; With the 2010 Amendments Adopted February 20, 2010; Effective June 1, 2010.

3. *Ethical Guidelines Sampler*, 4.

exploit persons over whom they have supervisory, evaluative, or other authority such as clients /patients, students, supervisees, research participants, and employees."[4] And both Codes specifically prohibit members from *exploiting* clients sexually. On the question of self-disclosure, to which we have earlier given considerable attention, the Australian Guidelines concede that there is "an absence of consensus regarding appropriate levels of self-disclosure of the psychologist to a client. Many psychologists believe that self-disclosure should be minimal while some argue that in certain circumstances the self-disclosure may promote positive outcomes for the client."[5]

We need now to examine the question of *testimony* in the light of the issues just discussed. With regard to the power held by the counselor, everything depends on the mutual respect that has developed between the counselor and the client. Respect, by its very nature, is non-invasive. The Christian counselor, if consistent with biblical norms, will be keen to see the autonomy of the client either preserved or enhanced, rather than being submerged. There will be no point in proceeding unless the client has appropriated attitudes, decisions, or modifications of personality genuinely, and with inner conviction, without undue dependence. While Jesus longed for people to put their trust in him, he issued his challenges and invitations, knowing that such people must retain the power to respond negatively, as in the memorable case of the rich young man (Matthew 19:16–22)

It may come as a surprise to know that, in principle, the follower of Jesus has *already* renounced power in personal interchange with other people. Having said this so boldly, cases may sometimes be quoted where this has not been so! Hence—and the Australian Code enjoins this—"it is particularly important that psychologists examine their motivations . . . the goal . . . should always be the welfare of the client."[6] The American Code spells the point out in greater detail, thus: "Psychologists are aware of and respect cultural, individual, and role differences, including those based on age, gender, gender identity, race, ethnicity, culture, national origin, religion, sexual orientation, disability, language and socio-economic status."[7]

At the risk of seeming defensive, in the last story related above, the client wanted to sample my perspective, but having done so, gave no indication that he had been convinced or swayed by it. Yes, it may be that he

4. *Ethical Principles*, 6.
5. *Ethical Guidelines Sampler*, 7.
6. Ibid., 7.
7. *Ethical Principles*,4.

had opened himself to hearing a new way of looking at things—a form of education, perhaps—but such would only add to his growing awareness of a new perspective. My motivation was that precisely this should happen!

Coming once again to the question of self-disclosure, I have indicated the benefits that I find in it, especially where it is *not* directly targeted on the problem-experiences of the client. The examples of self-disclosure given in the Australian Guidelines "include psychologists disclosing that they share, or have shared, a common problem, sexual orientation, or religious affiliation with the client."[8] Once again the welfare of the client is paramount and "self-disclosure should never be based on the psychologist's needs."[9]

Where the Christian psychologist actually *needs* to be displaying personal faith to a client, irrespective of *that person's needs*, then the priority given in the New Testament to the interests of the other has been turned on its head! Such a requirement is unfitting both from a Christian and a professional standpoint.

5. Ethical boundaries

The American Code deals with this question under the heading, *Conflict of Interest*, expressed as follows: "Psychologists refrain from taking on a professional role when personal, scientific, professional, legal, financial, or other interests or relationships could reasonably be expected to (1) impair their objectivity, competence, or effectiveness in performing their functions as psychologists, or (2) expose the person or organization with whom the professional relationship exists to harm or exploitation."[10] In their treatment of professional boundaries, the Australian Guidelines extract, as needing particular attention, the question of *boundary crossings and boundary violations*.

> "[Boundary] crossings are departures from commonly accepted practice that some psychologists may see as appropriate, for example attending a client's special event or borrowing a book from a client. It is acknowledged that both cultural background and theoretical orientation will influence how psychologists and their clients construe certain behaviours. Nevertheless, given that such boundary blurriness is often a precursor to later major transgressions, it is

---

8. *Ethical Guidelines Sampler*, 4.
9. Ibid.4.
10. *Ethical Principles*, 6.

important for the psychologist to examine the implications of such actions, no matter how innocuous they seem at the time."[11]

In discussing this issue, let us recognize that *Christianity gives rise necessarily to a distinctive theoretical orientation* with respect to professions and institutions involved in *the care of people*. This involves loving people, whatever their need, and whatever their age, race, or gender; and loving, not only in the sense of providing resources, but also in the sense of providing a warm and supportive environment. Many existing institutions, indeed, emerged from Christianity in the first place. It is entirely appropriate, however, that major responsibility should be taken over, in appropriate circumstances and at a later time, by any state or nation which embraces a commitment of care. It could now become possible, however, that the profession involved would develop its own theoretical orientation, differing from the original, which could become mandatory and exclusive, especially where financial assistance from the state is involved. Hence "boundary crossings" will vary with the culture or the sub-culture which provides their context, and so some caution is required when professional rulings are made. On the other hand, where a professional society discerns personal or social effects of certain behaviors and connects these with whatever motives are now seen to precede them, the Christian needs to take note of these connections rather than resenting or repudiating them, purely on the grounds of their novelty.

Having said this, where do we now stand on the question of what I have called "testimony"? Is a descriptive statement of the counselor's faith-position, in the course of normal and relevant conversational interchange, a "boundary crossing"? My view on this is that if the faith-statement were "at the ready" in the mind of the Christian counselor, such that it could be produced whenever there was a pretext for doing so, then it has become dislodged from a primary focus on the interests of the client. And we must admit that, from time to time, there are Cowboy (and Cowgirl) Christians around in the various helping professions, who have been confused or immature in their understanding of "help," and in the way they pursue it. It seems to me that, on the issue raised, each case should be judged on its own merits. As the Australian Guidelines admit, transgressions of various kinds do occur, and we must document these and learn from them. It would be a pity, however, if we were to place a complete embargo on verbal statements of the counselor's faith, without reference to motivation, context, or psychological impact.

11. *Ethical Guidelines Sampler*, 7.

6. Violating boundaries

So much for boundary crossings! The second issue discussed in the Australian Guidelines is on the question of *boundary violations*.

> *Family, personal or friendship relationships.* In such relationships there is a personal connection between the psychologist and client, such that the psychologist's private life is accessible to the client or a friendship bond exists between psychologist and client that either pre-dated the professional relationship and/or might be expected to continue after the professional relationship has ceased. Combining such relationships with a professional psychologist/client relationship is ethically problematic because they are generally long-term and/or have goals that are incompatible with a professional relationship.[12]

After careful reflection about this statement, it seems to me that the central issue here is *whether or not the psychologist is fully able to act in the best interests of a client when that client is also a friend.* In particular we need to ask what is at stake ethically when the psychologist's private life is accessible to the client. Is it that the access to the psychologist, enjoyed by the client-friend, lacks psychological insights when compared with the insights of the psychologist, thus bringing about what is basically a communication problem? Or is it that *the objectivity of the psychologist is compromised by the friendship?* (Perhaps friendship—like love—is blind; and friends—like lovers—cannot see the follies that they commit!) I think it is probably the latter alternative that is being targeted by the *Guidelines*. And if lack of objectivity has been shown to be the regular result in cases such as the client-friend, then the warning carries considerable weight.

However, it is by no means impossible that one friend—in this case the psychologist—can temporarily objectify the client-friend for the purpose of counseling him or her more effectively. Such situations are not at all uncommon in life, particularly when the ethics of one friend are brought to the attention of the other in a kindly, but critical way. A story about Sir Thomas More is appropriate here.

When the English king, Henry VIII, was demanding More's acquiescence to those policies concerning divorce which he knew More, in conscience, could not approve, More's wife begged her husband to compromise his principles so that she might not lose him. Weighing precisely

---

12. *Ethical Guidelines Sampler*, 7.

his responsibility to his wife with that of his conscience—surely a reflective exercise—and knowing what his decision would mean to her, he refused, upon which his wife was furious with him. Later, however, she not only accepted his decision, but realized that his moral reflections and decisions were largely what she loved in him. From the other side of the relationship, it would be most implausible to say that More had stopped loving his wife to allow himself to reflect about her. It would seem then that personal relationships may be of such a quality that they can encompass, within their scope, abstract or principled contemplation of one participant by the other. More's story is not everybody's story, however, and a refusal to compromise while in relationship, may, in many people, be the exception rather than the rule. We repeat, however, that a particular charge of boundary violation should be judged, as with a charge of boundary crossing, with reference to context, motivation, and psychological impact.

We return now to our earlier statement: that Christianity gives rise necessarily to a theoretical orientation with respect to professions and institutions involved in the care of people. Although there is considerable room to move within biblical theology itself, there are distinctive principles that emerge, along with cogent applications of these to everyday living; and it is important to observe whether or when such Christian principles dovetail with current guidelines, or alternatively would require certain modifications and amplifications.

C. DECLARATION

1. The urge, in the New Testament, to share "the good news"

At the heart of the Christian's faith is the good news that God, through his son Jesus, has made possible for any human being the forgiveness of sins, a reconciliation with God, and a personal transformation, the end-point of which will be a nature like Christ's. All of this is bound up in the term *gospel*.

After his resurrection, Jesus said to his disciples:

> . . . you will receive power when the Holy Spirit comes on you; and you will be my witnesses in Jerusalem, and in all Judea and Samaria, and to the ends of the earth. (Acts 1:8)

In response Paul, the great missionary and writer, declares:

> . . . Christ's love *compels* us, because we are convinced that one died for all, and therefore all died. And he died for all, that those who live should no longer live for themselves but for him who died for them and was raised again . . . Therefore, if anyone is in Christ, the new creation has come: The old has gone, the new is here! All this is from God, who reconciled us to himself through Christ and gave us the ministry of reconciliation: that God was reconciling the world to himself in Christ, not counting people's sins against them. And he has committed to us the message of reconciliation. *We are therefore Christ's ambassadors, as though God were making his appeal through us.* We implore you on Christ's behalf: *Be reconciled to God.* (2 Corinthians 5:14–20)

I have emphasized certain words in this passage to show how basic and how deep is the Christian's motivation to communicate the gospel. And one would expect that in any situation which potentially plumbs the depths of someone's personhood, the desire to share the gospel would be a strong one. Could it therefore be acceptable, within the range of counseling procedures, to take the initiative of *introducing* the Christian gospel to a client?

2. Declaration: three concerns

In attempting an answer, several issues must be examined. The first concerns the question: why did the client come to the counselor in the first place? Was it to gain relief from depression or anxiety? Was it to be released from the prison-house of obsessive-compulsive disorder? Was it to face post-traumatic stress disorder? And in the light of any one of these possibilities, has there been a discernible professional progress, during counseling, towards cure or, at least, some significant improvement? In other words, has the clinical task been faithfully addressed? If the answer is "No!" then the *witness* of the Christian counselor is at least doubtful, and any attempt at *declaration* would likely, from a Christian angle alone, appear hollow.

The second concerns the counselor's ability, before God, to be a worker who correctly handles "the word of truth," that is, the text of the Bible. An inexperienced Christian, for example, might seize on the story where Jesus heals a paralytic;[13] and point out that forgiveness came first and healing second, the implication being that any client must seek forgiveness before there is any chance of healing. Such a reading ignores

---

13. Matthew 9:1–7.

Profession

much of the significance of the total story, where Jesus is dealing simultaneously with the paralyzed man, his friends, and the teachers of the law who were watching the whole proceedings. The interpretation, then, is superficial and therefore dangerous.

The third is the situation in which the client, with no previous religious experience, is expecting to be treated in a thoroughly secular way, analogous to visiting a general practitioner in a medical practice. In this case, to introduce the Christian gospel could be seen as tantamount to ignoring or being disrespectful to the client's expectations.

In any of these three cases, the Christian counselor involved could be accused of being *invasive* or *intrusive*, because issues of an entirely new kind from those expected by and familiar to the client may seem to be foisted upon him or her, and that without introduction, without connection, and without permission. Such could cogently be called religious exploitation. It might then be argued back, from a Christian point of view, that there have been occasions through the years when the gospel has been preached "out of the blue" but still has penetrated the feelings and thoughts of the hearer. The important difference is that the latter "left-field" experiences have not occurred in structured professional situations, in which the person pays for the service and is given, at least on the contemporary scene, written indications of what is to be expected, along with a listing of the client's rights and privileges.

Having looked at these possibilities, the question remains whether it is ever acceptable for the counselor to take some initiative in presenting the Christian gospel to the client. At this point we need to explore a context in which the presentation of the gospel may be seen to be *relevant* to the aims of the counseling.

3. Declaration: clinical relevance?

Let us suppose that a male client is disturbed and distressed because, on account of an unsatisfactory relationship, he discovered himself perpetrating an action against another person which was plainly aggressive and cruel. In this scenario, however, there is no suggestion of any complaint or payback, with the result that fear of recrimination has been removed. The client, however, in processing both his own lifestyle and personal tendencies, has discerned a pattern wherein the aggressive motif was somehow built-in, "ready," as it were, to be appropriately triggered. Let us assume now that there has been careful examination of attachment patterns, and of other significant relationships, of current family, economic, and occupational pressures, and of the efficacy of present support structures, as well as the adequacy of his world view. In other words, let us imagine that all the procedures relevant to our diagnosis and regularly used in our practice have been implemented.

When all this has been seen and done, our client still finishes up with a burdened conscience, wearied by his guilt, and despairing of his efforts to find a new direction in life. From a Christian viewpoint, this *would* be an appropriate time to convey Jesus' invitation:

> Come to me, all you who are weary and burdened, and I will give you rest. Take my yoke upon you and learn from me, for I am gentle and humble in heart, and you will find rest for your souls. (Matthew 11:28, 29)

And it would be *intrinsic* to the client's problem; that is, the invitation would present something relevant to his distress, rather than something imposed upon the problem because of a generalized evangelistic commitment of the Christian counselor. Let us note also that the invitation given is not followed by a particular therapeutic guarantee or promise. What is offered is a *relationship with Christ* as spelled out in the New Testament. This does not imply immediate healing, but yet we recall some of the findings in previous chapters, whereby a mutual relationship would often generate elements of therapy.

D. SOME OPTIONS

1. Continuation of psychological services

Should the decision be taken to proceed as suggested above, the counselor should reveal to the client his or her personal commitment to Christianity, and to the view that there are resources within the Christian faith which could affect the client's development and make some contribution to the burdens being carried. Immediately after such a statement, however, *the counselor should ask the client's permission* to open up such a discussion. This is an extension of the Australian Code, Section A.3., which deals with "informed consent." Thus A.3.1.declares, *inter alia*:

> *Psychologists* fully inform *clients* regarding the psychological services they intend to provide.[14]

Similarly, from the American Code, but with greater helpful detail:

> When obtaining informed consent to therapy . . . psychologists inform clients/patients as early as is feasible in the therapeutic relationship *about the nature and anticipated course of therapy*, fees, involvement of third parties, and limits of confidentiality *and provide sufficient opportunity for the client/patient to ask questions and receive answers.*[15]

At this point, there could well be debate about whether resources within the Christian faith could be described as "psychological." In reply, it would be fair to point out, as has been done in previous chapters of this book, that the Scriptures of the Old and New Testaments have a great deal to say about human beings, along with the pressures, the internal resources, and the relationships which characterize their existence. And it is exciting to observe that recent and current theologians have coordinated these rather scattered contributions into schemata parallel to, and in some cases, critical of some modern formulations in psychology. Such defense as this may be unnecessary, however, in the light of the definitional issue now to be addressed.

In the section of the Australian Code dealing with definitions, *psychological service* is defined as follows:

> Psychological service means any service provided by a *psychologist* to a *client* **including but not limited to** professional activities, psychological activities, professional practice, teaching, supervision, research practice, professional services, and psychological procedures.[16]

In this connection, it should be pointed out that such a definition may or may not be congruent with the approach of the American Code.

Many respected publications refer to the psychological possibilities inherent in religion, but when these possibilities are described as *declarations*, sensitivities within the counseling profession may be stirred by the specter of uncontrolled proselytization. I have attempted to show that the presentation of the Christian good news bears, within itself, constraints of an ethical

---

14. *Australian Code of Ethics*, 13.
15. *Ethical Principles*, 13. My emphases.
16. *Australian Code of Ethics*, 10. Words marked in bold for emphasis.

kind, which deplore exploitation and are devoted to the interests of the client. Should this not prove convincing, however, there remains another option.

2. Termination of psychological services

Granted the steps taken by the counselor with the client, as indicated above in option 1, it might now transpire that the counselor, possibly advised by a senior colleague, becomes unsure that the move towards declaration fulfils the spirit of the Code. If a doubt on the issue remains, then in fairness to the counseling profession, either the offer to link the treatment of the client's problems to the Christian good news should be withdrawn, or the current psychological services should be terminated. Should termination be chosen, there would then be the possibility for the former client to pursue the Christian option with the former counselor outside the context of professional counseling.

It must be clear, however, that the role of *counseling*, so recently in place, must now be abandoned. A clandestine continuation of therapeutic-and-declarative activity would be tantamount to reinstalling, unofficially, what had been judged too difficult professionally. To do this would seem to involve an element of deception and possibly of bad faith.

A further implication of such a move is that both Codes require certain other procedures when termination has been decided. The following requirements seem relevant to the situation being envisaged. According to the American Code:

> Psychologists terminate therapy when it becomes reasonably clear that the client/patient no longer needs the service, is not likely to benefit, or is being harmed by continued service . . . Except where precluded by the actions of clients/patients or third-party payors, prior to termination psychologists provide pre-termination counseling and suggest alternative service providers as appropriate.[17]

Similarly in the Australian Code:

> When *psychologists* terminate a *professional relationship* with a *client*, they shall have due regard for the psychological processes inherent in the services being provided, and the psychological well-being of the *client*.

---

17. *Ethical Principles*, 14.

> *Psychologists* make reasonable arrangements for the continuity of service provision when they are no longer able to deliver the *psychological service.*[18]

Providing continuity of service is an obvious but important responsibility. However, a strong case could be made for recruiting a psychologist who would be in sympathy with the particular psychological processes inherent in the original counseling service. Once again, as both Codes declare, and the New Testament ethic requires, the wellbeing of the client will finally determine the choice of a continuing counselor.

E. CONCLUSION

In what has been argued above, it is my contention that, with the appropriate ethics in place, and with the recognition that Christianity would never countenance the desire to rob a client of autonomy or personal discretion, there need be no contradiction between the Codes, on the one hand, and the place of Christian witness, testimony, and declaration—as defined above—on the other. However, from the New Testament in general, and especially from Romans 13, Christians are required to give practical respect to decisions made by governing authorities; and if a secular view about counseling or anything else becomes mandatory, then—though in certain societies there may exist the privilege of debating decisions differing from their own—they must be prepared to negotiate, or, if need be, to comply, provided that to do so is not completely contrary to their deepest beliefs.

Having said this with sincerity, it remains important, whatever a Christian's occupation may be, to understand the way God has communicated with human beings: through Christ, who himself has been described as *the Word* (John 1:1–14) and also through *the written word*, the Scriptures, which are God-breathed (2 Timothy 3:16a). It is also important to absorb the full impact of the assertion made in the book of Hebrews about the impact of the Word of God upon human personality.

> *For the word of God is living and active. Sharper than any double-edged sword, it penetrates even to dividing soul and spirit, joints and marrow; it judges the thoughts and attitudes of the heart. Nothing in all creation is hidden from God's sight. Everything is uncovered and laid bare before the eyes of him to whom we must give account.*

---

18. *Australian Code of Ethics,* 23.

Walking Alongside

Therefore, since we have a great high priest who has ascended into heaven, Jesus the Son of God, let us hold firmly to the faith we profess. (Hebrew 4:12–14)

Walking: An Epilogue

In the Introduction to this book, the goal was to contribute some understanding of the major presuppositions that, for a Christian believer, bear upon the practice of the helping professions, and particularly of counseling. Thus chapters were devoted to the scriptural understanding of counsel; of people; of sin; of self-esteem; of God's continuing interaction with people, which was called Providence; of relationships in general, and then love in particular; of happiness; and lastly of inwardness. There was no suggestion that such presuppositions are necessarily absent from a non-Christian approach to counseling, but it was considered worthwhile to spell out in detail the wealth of scriptural material applying to each and all, as well as seeing them through the lens of Christian discipleship.

Because it was concluded that happiness is a by-product that emerges in the pursuit of an ultimately worthwhile goal, it is fair to ask *what such a worthwhile goal might be.*

Two answers have been given in the course of discussion. The first was to say that such a goal is not only *a process generating love within the personality of the counselor, walking alongside any person whatsoever* who needs or requests help; but also *a therapeutic process encouraging the development of love in counselees* which will suffuse those life-relationships, either within themselves or with others, which have previously proved difficult.

The second answer, which in its breadth encompasses the first, is *shalom*. As in the introduction to chapter 3, we find that this means "*universal flourishing, wholeness, and delight*—a rich state of affairs in which natural needs are satisfied and natural gifts fruitfully employed, a state of affairs which inspires joyful wonder as its Creator and Savior opens doors and welcomes the creatures in whom he delights. *Shalom*, in other words, *is the way things ought to be*."[1] It is in this direction *that we must be walking*.

How, then, can these lofty goals be brought within the compass of the ordinary counseling room? I think that chapter 10 gives some practical guidance on this point. Although it focuses upon the acceptability of a Christian approach within the counseling profession, it accompanies this with an analysis of the basic ways in which Christians profess their faith. This may help us to apply our ultimate goal within whichever helping profession we work. Thus "witness" points to that aspect of inner life that so permeates the speech and behavior of a Christian that it may well be noted by the person involved, and incorporated into his or her life and adjustment. And "testimony," given in the context either of appropriate self-disclosure, or by the truthful answering of a client's direct questions, will point in a similar direction. "Declaration," may or may not be a possibility, but if it is, it will reinforce and clarify the impact made by witness and testimony.

To function well and responsibly in one's profession is undoubtedly something that God wills and applauds. To have in mind appropriate wisdom from the helping disciplines and, in particular, from psychological and neurological research in our care for people requires continuing study, research, and consultation. This is, in small measure, tantamount to following in the footsteps of God's own creativity and inventiveness. We are also immensely favored because the Son of God himself lived our life and well knew our ups and downs.

As Jesus Christ abides in us through his Spirit, and we in him, we may walk alongside others, seeing their reality through the lens of scriptural understanding, and discerning also the Spirit-warmth within ourselves, transforming us to learn more and practice better.

---

1. Plantinga, *Not the Way It's Supposed To Be: A Breviary of Sin*, 10. (Emphasis in the last sentence is mine.)

Bibliography

American Psychiatric Association. *Diagnostic and Statistical Manual of Mental Disorders.* Fourth edition. Washington DC: American Psychiatric Association, 1994.
American Psychological Association. *Ethical Principles of Psychologists and Code of Conduct.* American Psychological Association, 2010.
Andersen, Bill. "God as a Person." *Interchange* 12 (1972) 213–27.
———. "Health of Personality" MA dissertation, University of Sydney, 1959.
Aristotle, *The Nichomachean Ethics.* Translated by J.A.K. Thomson as *The Ethics of Aristotle.* London: Penguin, 1955.
Australian Psychological Society. *Code of Ethics.* Melbourne: Australian Psychological Society Ltd., 2001.
———. *Ethical Guidelines Sampler.* Melbourne: Australian Psychological Society Ltd., 2005.
Bachelor, A., and A. Horvath "The Therapeutic Relationship." In *The Heart & Soul of Change,* edited by Hubble M.A. et al., 133–78. Washington DC: American Psychological Association, 2001.
Baptist Hymn Book. London: Novello, 1963.
Boff, Leonardo. *Holy Trinity, Perfect Community.* Translated by Phillip Berryman. Maryknoll, NY: Orbis Books, 2000.
Bonhoeffer, Dietrich. *Creation and Fall/Temptation: Two Biblical Studies.* Translated by J.C. Fletcher and E. Bethge. New York: Macmillan, 1952.
Braaten, C.E. and R.W. Jenson, eds. *Sin, Death and the Devil.* Grand Rapids: Eerdmans, 2000.
Brother Lawrence. *The Practice of the Presence of God.* London: Epworth, 1959.
Campbell, Alastair. *Encounter with God.* Bletchley, Milton Keynes: Scripture Union, 2009.
Carson, D.A. *The Difficult Doctrine of the Love of God.* Leicester: InterVarsity, 2000.
Charnock, Stephen. *Discourses upon the Existence and Attributes of God, Vol 1.* London: Religious Tract Society, 1839.
Contemporary English Version. Canberra: The Bible Society in Australia, 1995.
Crabb, Larry. *Effective Biblical Counseling.* Grand Rapids: Zondervan, 1977.
Dockery, David. "An Outline of Paul's View of the Spiritual Life: Foundation for an Evangelical Spirituality." In *Exploring Christian Spirituality: An Ecumenical Reader,* edited by K.J. Collins, 339–51. Grand Rapids: Baker, 2000.
Doidge, Norman. *The Brain that Changes Itself.* New York: Penguin, 2007.
Dotterer, R.H. *Philosophy by Way of the Sciences.* New York: Macmillan, 1935.

Bibliography

Elliott, Matthew. *Faithful Feelings: Emotion in the New Testament.* Leicester: InterVarsity, 2005.

Fallding, H.J. "Modern Christians in a Christianized Society." *Journal of Christian Education*, 50, 2 (2007) 23–31.

Flemming, Dean. *Contextualization in the New Testament.* Leicester: Apollos, 2005.

Franck, Johann, "Jesus, priceless treasure." In *The Baptist Hymn Book.* 851. London: Novello, 1963.

Glover, Richard. "Doing it tough for self-esteem." In *The Sydney Morning Herald: Spectrum.* March 1, 1997.

Green, Joel. *Body, Soul, and Human Life: The Nature of Humanity in the Bible.* Grand Rapids: Baker Academic, 2008.

Greenberg, R.P. "Common Psychosocial Factors in Psychiatric Drug Therapy." In *The Heart & Soul of Change*, edited by Hubble M.A. et al., 297–328. Washington DC: American Psychological Association, 2001.

Greenfield, S. *Tomorrow's people: How 21st-Century Technology Is Changing the Way We Think and Feel.* London: Penguin, 2003.

Grenz, S.J. *The Social God and the Relational Self.* Louisville: Westminster John Knox, 2001.

———. *Theology for the Community of God.* Grand Rapids: Eerdmans, 2000.

Gubbins, James P. "Positive Psychology: Friend or Foe of Religious and Virtue Ethics?" *Journal of the Society of Christian Ethics*, 28, 2 (2008) 181–203.

Happiness and Its Causes: Official Conference Guide. Sydney: Vayrayana Institute, 2009.

Hill, Brian V. "Mainstreaming Values Issues in Education." *Journal of Christian Education*, 39, 1, (1996) 7–16.

Hubble, M.A., et al. *The Heart & Soul of Change.* Washington DC: American Psychological Association, 2001.

Jewett, Robert. *Paul's Anthropological Terms.* Leiden: Brill, 1971.

Johnson, Aubrey. *The Vitality of the Individual in the Thought of Ancient Israel.* Second edition. Cardiff: University of Wales Press, 1964.

Jones, S.L., and R.E. Butman. *Modern Psychotherapies: A Comprehensive Christian Appraisal.* Downer's Grove: InterVarsity, 1991.

Kierkegaard, Søren. *Fear and Trembling.* Translated by Walter Lowrie. Princeton, NJ: Princeton University Press, 1974.

Kleinig, John. "Moral Education and the Nature of Morality." *Journal of Christian Education* 72, (1981) 31–45.

Lau, Mark A. *Mindfulness-Based Cognitive Therapy Workshop Tour 2009.* Heidelberg: CPM Training and Counselling, 2009.

Lewis, C.S. *The Abolition of Man.* London: Geoffrey Bles, 1947.

———. *The Screwtape Letters.* Rev.ed. New York: Collier, 1982.

———. *The Four Loves.* London: Collins, 1963.

Macquarie Dictionary Second Edition. Sydney: The Macquarie Library, 1992.

McGrath, Alister. *Bridge-Building: Effective Christian Apologetics.* Leicester: InterVarsity, 1992.

Meilaender, Gilbert. "I Renounce the Devil and All His Ways." In *Sin, Death and the Devil* edited by Carl E. Braaten and Robert W. Jenson, 76–93. Grand Rapids: Eerdmans, 2000.

Nathan, P.E. and J.M. Gorman, eds. *Treatments That Work.* Oxford: Oxford University Press, 1998.

Bibliography

Pannenberg, W. *Anthropology in Theological Perspective*. Philadelphia: Westminster, 1985.
Pedersen, Johannes. *Israel: Its Life and Culture*. Oxford: Cumberlege, 1926.
Peterson, Christopher and Martin E.P. Seligman. *Character Strengths and Virtues: A Handbook and Classification*. New York: Oxford University Press, 2004.
Peterson, E.H. *The Message*. Colorado Springs: NavPress, 2002.
Plantinga, Cornelius Jr. *Not the Way It's Supposed To Be: A Breviary of Sin*. Grand Rapids: Eerdmans, 1995.
Powers, John. *Introduction to Tibetan Buddhism*. Ithaca: Snow Lion, 1995.
Ridderbos, H. *Paul: An Outline of His Theology*. Grand Rapids: Eerdmans, 1973.
Roberts, Robert C. *Spirituality and Human Emotion.*, Grand Rapids: Eerdmans, 1982.
Robinson, J.A.T. *The Body*. London: S.C.M., 1952.
Rogers, Carl. *Client-Centered Therapy*. London: Constable, 2003.
Sanders, J. *The God Who Risks*. Downers Grove: InterVarsity, 1998.
Schuller, R. *Self-Esteem: The New Reformation*. Waco: Word Books, 1982.
Sears, Robert R. "A Theoretical Framework for Personality and Social Behavior." *American Psychologist* 6, 9 (1951) 476–82.
Shults, F.LeRon. *Reforming Theological Anthropology: After the Philosophical Turn to Relationality*. Grand Rapids: Eerdmans, 2003.
Siegel, Daniel J. *The Developing Mind*. New York: Guilford, 1999.
———. *The Mindful Brain*. New York: Norton, 2007.
Siegel, D.J., and M. Hartzell. *Parenting from the Inside Out: How a Deeper Self-Understanding Can Help You Raise Children Who Thrive*. New York: Penguin, 2003.
Skinner, B. *About Behaviorism*. New York: Vintage Books, 1976.
Sydney Symphony: 2009 Season: Great Classics., Sydney: 2009.
Today's New International Version Study Bible. Grand Rapids: Zondervan, 2006.
Twelftree, Graham H. *Christ Triumphant: Exorcism Then and Now*. London: Hodder & Stoughton, 1985.
———. *In the Name of Jesus: Exorcism among Early Christians*. Grand Rapids: Baker, 2007.
Volf, M. *Exclusion & Embrace*. Nashville: Abingdon Press, 1996.
———. *Free of Charge: Giving and Forgiving in a Culture Stripped of Grace*. Grand Rapids: Zondervan, 2005.
Way, Arthur. *The Letters of St Paul*, London: Marshall Morgan & Scott, 1901.
Williams, Mark et al. *The Mindful Way through Depression: Freeing Yourself from Chronic Unhappiness*. New York: Guilford, 2007.
Wolff, H.W. *Anthropology of the Old Testament*. Translated by Margaret Kohl. Philadelphia: Philadelphia Fortress Press, 1974.
Wolterstorff, Nicholas. *Until Justice and Peace Embrace*. Grand Rapids: Eerdmans, 1975.
Yarhouse, M.A. et al. *Modern Psychopathologies*. Downers Grove: InterVarsity, 2005.
Zeig, K.J. ed. *The Evolution of Psychotherapy*. New York: Brunner/Mazel, 1987.
Zhong, B.S.L. "Expanding the Understanding of Mindfulness: Seeing the Tree and the Forest." *The Humanist Psychologist* 37 (2009) 117–36.

www.ingramcontent.com/pod-product-compliance
Lightning Source LLC
Chambersburg PA
CBHW051801230426
43670CB00012B/2380